SLOW-COOKER

CLASSICS

Contents

Piping Hot Soups

Easy Vegetarian Vegetable Bean Soup

Cook Time: 8½ hours

3 cans (14 ounces each) vegetable broth

2 cups cubed unpeeled potatoes

2 cups sliced leeks, white part only (about 3 medium)

1 can (14½ ounces) diced tomatoes, undrained

1 medium onion, chopped

1 cup chopped or shredded cabbage

1 cup sliced celery

1 cup sliced carrots

3 cloves garlic, chopped

⅛ teaspoon dried rosemary

1 can (16 ounces) white beans, rinsed and drained

Salt and black pepper

1. Combine broth, potatoes, leeks, tomatoes with juice, onion, cabbage, celery carrots, garlic and rosemary in 5-quart slow cooker.

2. Cover; cook on LOW 8 hours.

3. Stir in beans and season with salt and pepper. Cover; cook about 30 minutes or until beans are heated through.

Makes 10 servings

Minestrone alla Milanese

2 cans (14½ ounces each) reduced-sodium beef broth

1 can (14½ ounces) diced tomatoes, undrained

1 cup diced potato

1 cup coarsely chopped green cabbage

1 cup coarsely chopped carrots

1 cup sliced zucchini

¾ cup chopped onion

¾ cup sliced fresh green beans

¾ cup coarsely chopped celery

¾ cup water

2 tablespoons olive oil

1 clove garlic, minced

½ teaspoon dried basil

¼ teaspoon dried rosemary

1 bay leaf

1 can (about 15 ounces) cannellini beans, rinsed and drained

Grated Parmesan cheese (optional)

1. Combine broth, tomatoes with juice, potato, cabbage, carrots, zucchini, onion, green beans, celery, water, oil, garlic, basil, rosemary and bay leaf in 5-quart slow cooker; mix well. Cover and cook on LOW 5 to 6 hours.

2. Add beans. Cover and cook on LOW 1 hour or until vegetables are tender.

3. Remove and discard bay leaf. Garnish with cheese, if desired.   *Makes 8 to 10 servings*

Pasta Fagioli Soup

Prep Time: 12 minutes   **Cook Time:** 4 to 5 hours

2 cans (14½ ounces each) reduced-sodium beef broth

1 can (15 ounces) Great Northern beans, rinsed and drained

1 can (14½ ounces) diced tomatoes, undrained

2 medium zucchini, quartered lengthwise and sliced

1 tablespoon olive oil

1½ teaspoons minced garlic

½ teaspoon dried basil

½ teaspoon dried oregano

½ cup uncooked tubetti, ditilini or small shell pasta

½ cup garlic-flavored croutons

½ cup grated Asiago or Romano cheese

3 tablespoons chopped fresh basil or Italian parsley (optional)

1. Combine broth, beans, tomatoes with juice, zucchini, oil, garlic, basil and oregano in slow cooker; mix well. Cover; cook on LOW 3 to 4 hours.

2. Stir in pasta. Cover; cook on LOW 1 hour or until pasta is tender.

3. Serve soup with croutons and cheese. Garnish with fresh basil, if desired.

Makes 5 to 6 servings

Navy Bean Bacon Chowder

Cook Time: 8¼ to 9¼ hours

1½ cups dried navy beans, rinsed and sorted

2 cups cold water

6 slices thick-cut bacon

1 medium carrot, cut lengthwise into halves, then cut into 1-inch pieces

1 small turnip, cut into 1-inch pieces

1 rib celery, chopped

1 medium onion, chopped

1 teaspoon dried Italian seasoning

⅛ teaspoon black pepper

1 can (46 ounces) reduced-sodium chicken broth

1 cup milk

1. Soak beans overnight in cold water; drain.

2. Cook bacon in medium skillet over medium heat. Drain fat; crumble bacon.

3. Combine beans, bacon, carrot, turnip, celery, onion, Italian seasoning and pepper in slow cooker. Add broth. Cover; cook on LOW 8 to 9 hours or until beans are tender.

4. Ladle 2 cups of soup mixture into food processor or blender. Process until smooth; return to slow cooker. Add milk. Cover; cook on HIGH 15 minutes or until heated through.

Makes 6 servings

Simmering Hot & Sour Soup

Prep Time: 10 to 15 minutes   **Cook Time:** 3¼ to 4¼ hours

2 cans (14½ ounces each)
  chicken broth

1 cup chopped cooked chicken
  or pork

4 ounces fresh shiitake
  mushroom caps, thinly
  sliced

½ cup sliced bamboo shoots, cut
  into thin strips

3 tablespoons rice wine vinegar

2 tablespoons soy sauce

1½ teaspoons Chinese chili paste
  or 1 teaspoon hot chili oil

4 ounces firm tofu, well drained
  and cut into ½-inch pieces

2 teaspoons dark sesame oil

2 tablespoons cornstarch

2 tablespoons cold water

  Chopped cilantro or sliced
  green onions

1. Combine chicken broth, chicken, mushrooms, bamboo shoots, vinegar, soy sauce and chili paste in slow cooker. Cover; cook on LOW 3 to 4 hours.

2. Stir in tofu and sesame oil. Blend cornstarch and water until smooth. Stir into slow cooker. Cover; cook on HIGH 15 minutes or until soup is thickened.

3. Serve hot; garnish with cilantro.

Makes 4 servings

Note: Dark or Asian sesame oil has a strong, nutty flavor so use it sparingly. Look for it in the Asian section of your supermarket or in specialty food shops.

Savory Pea Soup with Sausage

Cook Time: 4 to 5 hours

8 ounces smoked sausage, cut lengthwise into halves, then cut into ½-inch pieces

3 medium carrots, sliced

1 package (16 ounces) dried split peas, rinsed and sorted

2 ribs celery, sliced

1 medium onion, chopped

¾ teaspoon dried marjoram

1 bay leaf

2 cans (14½ ounces each) reduced-sodium chicken broth

1. Heat medium nonstick skillet over medium heat. Add sausage; cook 5 to 8 minutes or until browned. Drain fat. Combine sausage, carrots, peas, celery, onion, marjoram and bay leaf in slow cooker. Pour broth over mixture.

2. Cover; cook on LOW 4 to 5 hours or until peas are tender. Remove and discard bay leaf. Cover; let stand 15 minutes to thicken.

Makes 6 servings

Beef, Barley & Onion Soup

Prep Time: 20 minutes   **Cook Time:** 8 hours

2 pounds beef stew meat, cut into ½-inch cubes

3 large carrots, cut into ½-inch-thick slices

2 large ribs celery, cut into ½-inch-thick slices

4 cans (14½ ounces each) beef broth

½ teaspoon dried oregano leaves

½ teaspoon salt

¼ teaspoon ground black pepper

½ cup barley

2 cups *French's*® French Fried Onions, divided

1. Combine beef, carrots, celery, broth and seasonings in slow cooker. Cover; cook on LOW setting for 7 hours (or on HIGH for 3½ hours) until meat and vegetables are tender.

2. Stir in barley. Cover and cook on LOW setting for 1 hour (or on HIGH for ½ hour) until barley is tender. Stir in *1 cup* French Fried Onions. Spoon soup into serving bowls; sprinkle with remaining onions.

Makes 8 servings

Note: Cook times vary depending on type of slow cooker used. Check manufacturer's recommendations for cooking beef and barley.

Mediterranean Lentil Soup

2 tablespoons olive oil

1 large onion, diced

1 stalk celery, chopped

2 large cloves garlic, finely minced

1 can (28 ounces) plum tomatoes, drained and chopped

1½ cups dried lentils, soaked in cold water 1 hour, drained and rinsed*

1 tablespoon tomato paste

1½ teaspoons dried thyme

6 cups beef broth

2 bay leaves

Vinaigrette

¾ cup packed fresh basil leaves

⅓ cup olive oil

2 tablespoons minced fresh parsley

2 tablespoons red wine vinegar

Salt and black pepper

Add 1 to 2 hours to cooking time if lentils are not soaked.

1. Heat 2 tablespoons oil in large saucepan over medium heat. Add onion, celery and garlic; cook and stir 5 minutes. Stir in tomatoes, lentils, tomato paste and thyme. Combine lentil mixture, broth and bay leaves in slow cooker; mix well.

2. Cover; cook on LOW 8 hours or on HIGH 4 hours or until lentils are soft.

3. Meanwhile, prepare vinaigrette. Combine basil, ⅓ cup oil, parsley and vinegar in blender or food processor. Blend until smooth. Stir vinaigrette into soup just before serving. Season with salt and pepper.

Makes 4 to 6 servings

Variation: Alternatively, place all soup ingredients except vinaigrette in slow cooker; mix well. Cover; cook on LOW 9 hours or on HIGH 4½ hours.

French Onion Soup

Prep Time: 30 minutes   **Cook Time:** 8 hours

4 tablespoons butter, divided

3 pounds yellow onions, sliced

1 tablespoon sugar

2 to 3 tablespoons dry white
  wine or water (optional)

2 quarts (8 cups) beef broth

8 to 16 slices French bread

½ cup (2 ounces) shredded
  Gruyère or Swiss cheese

1. Melt butter in large skillet over medium to low heat. Add onions; cover and cook just until onions are tender and transparent, but not browned, about 10 minutes.

2. Remove cover. Sprinkle sugar over onions. Cook, stirring, 8 to 10 minutes or until onions are caramelized. Scrape onions and any browned bits into 4-quart slow cooker. If desired, add wine to skillet. Bring to a boil; scrape up any browned bits with a wooden spoon. Add to slow cooker. Stir in broth. Cover; cook on LOW 8 hours or on HIGH 6 hours.

3. Preheat broiler. To serve, ladle soup into individual soup bowls; top with 1 or 2 slices bread and about 1 tablespoon cheese. Place under broiler until cheese is melted and bubbly.   *Makes 8 servings*

Variation: Substitute 1 cup dry white wine for 1 cup beef broth.

Sweet and Sour Cabbage Soup

Cook Time: 6 to 8 hours

2 pounds boneless chuck roast

1 can (28 ounces) tomatoes, cut into pieces, undrained

1 can (15 ounces) tomato sauce

1 large onion, thinly sliced

3 carrots, shredded

2 pounds green cabbage, shredded

4 cups water

¾ cup sugar

½ cup lemon juice

1 tablespoon caraway seeds

2 teaspoons salt

1 teaspoon pepper

1. Cut chuck roast into 4 pieces. Spray 12-inch skillet with cooking spray. Heat over medium-high heat until hot. Brown roast on both sides. Place in 4-quart slow cooker.

2. Add tomatoes with juice, tomato sauce, onion, carrots, cabbage, water, sugar, lemon juice, caraway seeds, salt and pepper. Cover; cook on LOW 6 to 8 hours or until meat is tender.

3. Remove beef from slow cooker. Shred beef and return to slow cooker; mix well.

Makes 8 to 10 servings

Hearty Mushroom and Barley Soup

Cook Time: 4 to 6 hours

9 cups chicken broth

1 package (16 ounces) button mushrooms, sliced

1 large onion, chopped

2 carrots, chopped

2 ribs celery, chopped

½ cup pearled barley

½ ounce dried porcini mushrooms

3 cloves garlic, minced

1 teaspoon salt

½ teaspoon dried thyme

½ teaspoon black pepper

Combine broth, button mushrooms, onion, carrots, celery, barley, porcini mushrooms, garlic, salt, thyme and pepper in 5-quart slow cooker; stir until well blended. Cover; cook on LOW 4 to 6 hours.

Makes 8 to 10 servings

Variation: Add a beef or ham bone to slow cooker with the rest of the ingredients. It adds more flavor to the soup.

Favorite Beef

Hearty Chili Mac

Cook Time: 5 hours

1 pound 90% lean ground beef

1 can (14½ ounces) diced
   tomatoes, drained

1 cup chopped onion

1 clove garlic, minced

1 tablespoon chili powder

½ teaspoon salt

½ teaspoon ground cumin

½ teaspoon dried oregano

¼ teaspoon red pepper flakes

¼ teaspoon black pepper

2 cups cooked macaroni

1. Brown ground beef in large nonstick skillet over medium-high heat, stirring to break up meat. Drain fat. Add tomatoes, onion, garlic, chili powder, salt, cumin, oregano, pepper flakes and black pepper to slow cooker; mix well.

2. Cover; cook on LOW 4 hours.

3. Stir in macaroni. Cover; cook 30 to 45 minutes or until macaroni is hot.

Makes 4 servings

Barbecued Meatballs

Prep Time: 35 minutes   **Cook Time:** 4 hours

2 pounds 95% lean ground beef

1⅓ cups ketchup, divided

3 tablespoons seasoned dry
   bread crumbs

1 egg, lightly beaten

2 tablespoons dried onion flakes

¾ teaspoon garlic salt

½ teaspoon black pepper

1 cup packed light brown sugar

1 can (6 ounces) tomato paste

¼ cup reduced-sodium soy sauce

¼ cup cider vinegar

1½ teaspoons hot pepper sauce

   Diced bell peppers (optional)

1. Preheat oven to 350°F. Combine ground beef, ⅓ cup ketchup, bread crumbs, egg, onion flakes, garlic salt and black pepper in medium bowl. Mix lightly but thoroughly; shape into 1-inch meatballs. Place meatballs in two 15×10-inch jelly-roll pans or shallow roasting pans. Bake 18 minutes or until browned. Transfer meatballs to slow cooker.

2. Mix remaining 1 cup ketchup, sugar, tomato paste, soy sauce, vinegar and hot pepper sauce in medium bowl. Pour over meatballs. Cover; cook on LOW 4 hours. Serve with cocktail picks. Garnish with diced bell peppers, if desired.

Makes about 4 dozen meatballs

Barbecued Franks: Arrange 2 (12-ounce) packages or 3 (8-ounce) packages cocktail franks in slow cooker. Combine 1 cup ketchup with brown sugar, tomato paste, soy sauce, vinegar and hot pepper sauce in medium bowl; pour over franks. Cook according to directions for Barbecued Meatballs.

Slow Cooker Rouladen

Cook Time: 8 to 10 hours

12 pieces top round beef,
    pounded thin (¼-inch thick)

Salt and black pepper

Garlic pepper

4 tablespoons Dijon mustard

1½ cups chopped onions

1½ cups chopped dill pickles

Nonstick cooking spray

¼ cup (½ stick) butter

5 tablespoons all-purpose flour

2 cans (14½ ounces each) beef
    broth

1 pound baby carrots

4 stalks celery, cut into 1-inch
    pieces

1. Place 1 piece of beef on cutting board; season with salt, black pepper and garlic pepper. Spread with 1 teaspoon mustard; top with 2 tablespoons each onion and pickles. Starting at one short side of beef fold about ⅓ of slice over on itself, tuck in long sides, then roll tightly. Secure with toothpick. Repeat with remaining slices of beef, salt, pepper, garlic pepper, onions and pickles.

2. Spray large nonstick skillet with cooking spray. Brown beef rolls in batches over medium-high heat until browned on all sides. Remove from skillet.

3. In same skillet, melt butter. Add flour; cook and stir 1 minute. Add beef broth, stirring constantly. Cook and stir until mixture thickens.

4. Pour half of broth mixture into slow cooker. Add beef rolls; cover with remaining broth mixture. Top with carrots and celery.

5. Cover; cook on LOW 8 to 10 hours or on HIGH 4 to 5 hours until beef is tender.

Makes 6 to 8 servings

Beef and Parsnip Stroganoff

Cook Time: 4½ to 5 hours

1 beef bouillon cube

¾ cup boiling water

1 boneless beef top round steak (about ¾ pound), trimmed

Nonstick olive oil cooking spray

2 cups cubed peeled parsnips

1 medium onion, halved and thinly sliced

¾ pound mushrooms, sliced

2 teaspoons minced garlic

¼ teaspoon black pepper

¼ cup water

1 tablespoon plus 1½ teaspoons all-purpose flour

3 tablespoons sour cream

1½ teaspoons Dijon mustard

¼ teaspoon cornstarch

1 tablespoon chopped fresh parsley

4 ounces uncooked wide noodles, drained and kept hot

1. Dissolve bouillon cube in ¾ cup boiling water; cool. Meanwhile, cut steak lengthwise in half, then crosswise into ½-inch strips. Spray large nonstick skillet with cooking spray; heat over high heat. Add beef; cook and stir about 4 minutes or until meat begins to brown. Transfer beef and juices to slow cooker.

2. Spray same skillet with cooking spray; heat over high heat. Add parsnips and onion; cook and stir about 4 minutes or until browned. Add mushrooms, garlic and pepper; cook and stir about 5 minutes or until mushrooms are tender. Transfer mixture to slow cooker.

3. Whisk ¼ cup water into flour in small bowl until smooth. Combine flour mixture and cooled bouillon in slow cooker; stir until blended. Cover; cook on LOW 4½ to 5 hours or until beef and parsnips are tender.

4. Turn off slow cooker. Remove beef and vegetables with slotted spoon to large bowl; reserve cooking liquid from beef. Blend sour cream, mustard and cornstarch in medium bowl. Gradually add reserved liquid to sour cream mixture; stir well to blend. Stir sour cream mixture into beef and vegetable mixture. Sprinkle with parsley; serve over hot noodles. Garnish, if desired. *Makes 4 servings*

Texas-Style Barbecued Brisket

Cook Time: 8 hours

1 beef brisket (3 to 4 pounds)

3 tablespoons Worcestershire sauce

1 tablespoon chili powder

1 teaspoon celery salt

1 teaspoon black pepper

1 teaspoon liquid smoke

2 cloves garlic, minced

2 bay leaves

Barbecue Sauce (recipe follows)

1. Trim excess fat from meat and discard. Place meat in resealable plastic food storage bag. Combine Worcestershire sauce, chili powder, celery salt, pepper, liquid smoke and garlic in small bowl. Spread mixture on all sides of meat; seal bag. Refrigerate 24 hours.

2. Place meat, marinade and bay leaves in 4-quart slow cooker, cutting meat in half, if necessary, to fit into slow cooker. Cover; cook on LOW 7 hours. Meanwhile, prepare Barbecue Sauce.

3. Remove meat from slow cooker and pour juices into 2-cup measure; let stand 5 minutes. Skim fat from juices. Remove and discard bay leaves. Stir 1 cup defatted juices into Barbecue Sauce. Discard remaining juices.

4. Return meat and barbecue sauce mixture to slow cooker. Cover; cook on LOW 1 hour or until meat is fork-tender. Cut across grain into ¼-inch-thick slices. Serve with barbecue sauce.

Makes 10 to 12 servings

Barbecue Sauce: Heat 2 tablespoons vegetable oil in medium saucepan over medium heat. Add 1 cup chopped onion and 1 teaspoon minced garlic; cook and stir 3 to 4 minutes. Add 1 cup ketchup, ½ cup molasses, ¼ cup cider vinegar, 2 teaspoons chili powder and ½ teaspoon dry mustard; simmer 5 minutes. Makes 1¾ cups sauce.

Easy Slow-Cooked Chili

Prep Time: 10 minutes   **Cook Time:** 6 hours

2 pounds lean ground beef

2 tablespoons chili powder

1 tablespoon ground cumin

1 can (28 ounces) crushed
   tomatoes in purée,
   undrained

1 can (15 ounces) red kidney
   beans, drained and rinsed

1 cup water

2 cups *French's®* French Fried
   Onions, divided

¼ cup *Frank's® RedHot®* Original
   Cayenne Pepper Sauce

  Sour cream and shredded
   Cheddar cheese

1. Cook ground beef, chili powder and cumin in large nonstick skillet over medium heat until browned, stirring frequently; drain. Transfer to slow cooker.

2. Stir in tomatoes with juice, beans, water, *½ cup* French Fried Onions and ***Frank's RedHot*** Sauce.

3. Cover; cook on LOW setting for 6 hours (or on HIGH for 3 hours). Serve chili topped with sour cream, cheese and remaining onions.   *Makes 8 servings*

Variation: For added Cheddar flavor, substitute *French's®* **Cheddar French Fried Onions** for the original flavor.

Beef and Vegetables in Rich Burgundy Sauce

Cook Time: 8¼ to 10¼ hours

1 package (8 ounces) baby carrots

1 package (8 ounces) sliced mushrooms

1 medium green bell pepper, cut into thin strips

1 boneless beef chuck roast (2½ pounds)

1 can (10½ ounces) condensed golden mushroom soup, undiluted

¼ cup dry red wine or beef broth

1 tablespoon Worcestershire sauce

1 package (1 ounce) dry onion soup mix

¼ teaspoon black pepper

3 tablespoons cornstarch

2 tablespoons water

4 cups hot cooked noodles

Chopped fresh parsley (optional)

1. Place carrots, mushrooms and bell pepper in slow cooker. Place roast on top of vegetables. Combine mushroom soup, wine, Worcestershire sauce, soup mix and black pepper in medium bowl; mix well. Pour soup mixture over roast. Cover; cook on LOW 8 to 10 hours.

2. Transfer roast to cutting board; cover with foil. Let stand 10 to 15 minutes before slicing.

3. Blend cornstarch and water until smooth; stir into slow cooker. Cook, uncovered, 15 minutes or until thickened. Serve beef and vegetables with sauce over cooked noodles. Garnish with parsley, if desired.

Makes 6 to 8 servings

Slow Cooker Brisket of Beef

Cook Time: 8 to 9 hours

1 whole well-trimmed beef
  brisket (about 5 pounds)

2 teaspoons minced garlic

½ teaspoon black pepper

2 large onions, cut into ¼-inch
  slices and separated into
  rings

1 bottle (12 ounces) chili sauce

1½ cups beef broth, dark ale or
  water

2 tablespoons Worcestershire
  sauce

1 tablespoon packed brown
  sugar

1. Place brisket, fat side down, in 5-quart slow cooker. Spread garlic evenly over brisket; sprinkle with pepper. Arrange onions over brisket. Combine chili sauce, broth, Worcestershire sauce and sugar; pour over brisket and onions. Cover and cook on LOW for 8 hours.

2. Turn brisket over; stir onions into sauce and spoon over brisket. Cover; cook until fork-tender. Transfer brisket to cutting board. Tent with foil; let stand 10 minutes.*

3. Stir juices in slow cooker. Discard fat from juices. (Juices may be thinned to desired consistency with water or thickened by simmering, uncovered, in saucepan.) Carve brisket across grain into thin slices. Spoon juices over brisket. *Makes 10 to 12 servings*

At this point, brisket may be covered and refrigerated up to one day before serving. To reheat brisket, cut diagonally into thin slices. Place brisket slices and juice in large skillet. Cover and cook over medium-low heat until heated through.

Tip: If desired, stir diced red boiling potatoes, sliced carrots, sliced parsnips or turnips into juices during last 2 hours of cooking time.

Favorite Beef Stew

Cook Time: 8¼ to 9¼ hours

3 carrots, cut lengthwise into halves, then cut into 1-inch pieces

3 ribs celery, cut into 1-inch pieces

2 large potatoes, peeled and cut into ½-inch pieces

1½ cups chopped onions

3 cloves garlic, chopped

4½ teaspoons Worcestershire sauce

¾ teaspoon dried thyme

¾ teaspoon dried basil

½ teaspoon black pepper

1 bay leaf

2 pounds beef for stew, cut into 1-inch pieces

1 can (14½ ounces) diced tomatoes, undrained

1 can (14½ ounces) reduced-sodium beef broth

½ cup cold water

¼ cup all-purpose flour

1. Layer ingredients in slow cooker in the following order: carrots, celery, potatoes, onions, garlic, Worcestershire sauce, thyme, basil, pepper, bay leaf, beef, tomatoes with juice and broth.

2. Cover and cook on LOW 8 to 9 hours.

3. Remove beef and vegetables to large serving bowl; cover and keep warm. Remove and discard bay leaf. Increase heat to HIGH. Blend water and flour in small bowl until smooth. Add ½ cup cooking liquid; mix well. Stir flour mixture into slow cooker. Cover and cook 15 minutes or until thickened. Pour sauce over meat and vegetables. Serve immediately.

Makes 6 to 8 servings

Spicy Beef and Pepper Fajitas

Prep Time: 10 minutes   **Cook Time:** 8 to 10 hours

1 beef flank steak (about
     1½ pounds), cut into
     6 pieces

1 cup chopped onion

2 medium green bell peppers,
     cut into ½-inch-wide strips

1 jalapeño pepper,* chopped

2 tablespoons chopped fresh
     cilantro

2 cloves garlic, minced

1 teaspoon chili powder

1 teaspoon ground cumin

½ teaspoon salt

¼ teaspoon ground red pepper

1 can (8 ounces) chopped
     tomatoes, drained

12 (7-inch) flour tortillas

     Toppings, such as sour cream,
          shredded Cheddar cheese
          and salsa (optional)

     Sliced avocado (optional)

*Jalapeño peppers can sting and irritate
the skin. Wear rubber gloves when
handling peppers and do not touch
eyes. Wash hands after handling.

1. Combine beef, onion, bell peppers, jalapeño pepper, cilantro, garlic, chili powder, cumin, salt and ground red pepper in slow cooker. Add tomatoes. Cover; cook on LOW 8 to 10 hours.

2. Remove beef from slow cooker and pull into shreds with fork. Return beef to slow cooker. To serve, layer beef mixture on tortillas. Top with toppings, if desired; roll up tortillas. Serve with sliced avocado, if desired.

Makes 12 servings

Corned Beef & Cabbage with Horseradish Mustard Sauce

Cook Time: 8½ to 9½ hours

1 large onion, cut into chunks

1½ cups baby carrots

16 small (1-inch) red potatoes, (about 1¼ pounds)*

1 corned beef brisket (2 to 2½ pounds)

½ large head cabbage (1 pound), cut into 8 thin wedges

⅓ cup sour cream

⅓ cup mayonnaise

2 tablespoons Dijon mustard

2 tablespoons prepared horseradish

If 1-inch potatoes are not available, use larger sizes and cut in halves or quarters, as needed.

1. Coat slow cooker with cooking spray. Place onion, carrots and potatoes in bottom of 4- to 5-quart slow cooker. Drain corned beef, reserving spice packet and juices from package. Place corned beef over vegetables; pour juices over beef and top with contents of spice packet. Add enough water to barely cover beef and vegetables (about 4 cups). Cover and cook on LOW 8 to 9 hours or on HIGH 5 to 6 hours, or until corned beef is fork-tender.

2. Transfer corned beef to large sheet of heavy-duty foil; wrap tightly and set aside. Add cabbage wedges to vegetables, pushing down into liquid. Turn heat to HIGH; cover and cook 30 to 40 minutes or until vegetables are tender.

3. Meanwhile, combine sour cream, mayonnaise, mustard and horseradish; mix well. Reserve ½ cup of the juices in slow cooker. Drain vegetables; transfer to serving platter. Thinly slice corned beef; arrange on platter and drizzle reserved juices over all. Serve with horseradish mustard sauce.

Makes 6 to 8 servings

Pleasing Pork

Pork Meatballs & Sauerkraut

Prep Time: 30 minutes   **Cook Time:** 6 to 8 hours

1¼ pounds lean ground pork

¾ cup dry bread crumbs

1 egg, lightly beaten

2 tablespoons milk

2 teaspoons caraway seeds, divided

1 teaspoon salt

½ teaspoon Worcestershire sauce

¼ teaspoon black pepper

1 jar (32 ounces) sauerkraut, drained, squeezed dry and snipped

½ cup chopped onion

6 slices bacon, crisp-cooked and crumbled

Chopped parsley

1. Combine ground pork, bread crumbs, egg, milk, 1 teaspoon caraway seeds, salt, Worcestershire sauce and pepper in large bowl. Shape mixture into 2-inch balls. Brown meatballs in large nonstick skillet over medium-high heat.

2. Combine sauerkraut, onion, bacon and remaining 1 teaspoon caraway seeds in slow cooker. Place meatballs on top of sauerkraut mixture.

3. Cover; cook on LOW 6 to 8 hours. Sprinkle with chopped parsley.

Makes 4 to 6 servings

Ale'd Pork and Sauerkraut

Cook Time: 6 hours (HIGH)

1 jar (32 ounces) sauerkraut, undrained

1½ tablespoons sugar

1 can (12 ounces) dark beer or ale

3½ pounds boneless pork shoulder or pork butt roast

½ teaspoon salt

¼ teaspoon garlic powder

¼ teaspoon black pepper

Paprika

1. Place sauerkraut in 5-quart slow cooker. Sprinkle with sugar; add beer. Place pork, fat side up, on top of sauerkraut mixture; sprinkle evenly with remaining ingredients.

2. Cover; cook on HIGH 6 hours.

3. Remove pork to serving platter. Remove sauerkraut with slotted spoon; arrange around pork. Spoon ½ to ¾ cup cooking liquid over sauerkraut. *Makes 6 to 8 servings*

Dijon Pork Roast with Cranberries

Prep Time: 10 minutes   **Cook Time:** 4 to 6 hours

¼ teaspoon ground allspice

¼ teaspoon salt

¼ teaspoon ground black pepper

1 boneless pork loin roast (2 to 2½ pounds), trimmed of excess fat

2 tablespoons *French's*® Honey Dijon Mustard

2 tablespoons honey

2 teaspoons grated orange peel

1⅓ cups *French's*® French Fried Onions, divided

1 cup dried cranberries

1. Combine allspice, salt and pepper; sprinkle over roast. Place meat in slow cooker. Blend mustard, honey and orange peel; pour over roast. Sprinkle with ⅔ *cup* French Fried Onions and cranberries.

2. Cover and cook on LOW setting for 4 to 6 hours (or on HIGH for 2 to 3 hours) until meat is fork-tender.

3. Remove pork to serving platter. Skim fat from sauce in slow cooker; transfer sauce to serving bowl. Slice meat and serve with fruit sauce; sprinkle with remaining onions.

Makes 6 servings

Note: Cook times vary depending on type of slow cooker used. Check manufacturer's recommendations for cooking pork roast.

Brats in Beer

1½ pounds bratwurst (about 5 or 6 links)

1 bottle (12 ounces) amber ale

1 medium onion, thinly sliced

2 tablespoons packed brown sugar

2 tablespoons red wine or cider vinegar

Spicy brown mustard

Cocktail rye bread

1. Combine bratwurst, ale, onion, brown sugar and vinegar in slow cooker.

2. Cover; cook on LOW 4 to 5 hours.

3. Remove bratwurst from cooking liquid. Cut into ½-inch-thick slices. For mini open-faced sandwiches, spread mustard on cocktail rye bread. Top with bratwurst slices and onion, if desired.

Makes 30 to 36 appetizers

Tip: Choose a light-tasting beer for cooking brats. Hearty ales might leave the meat tasting slightly bitter.

Autumn Vegetables and Pork Chops

6 pork chops, ¾-inch thick

1 medium-size acorn squash

¾ cup packed brown sugar

3 tablespoons chopped green onion

2 tablespoons butter, melted

2 tablespoons orange juice

1 teaspoon Worcestershire sauce

1 teaspoon grated orange peel

¼ teaspoon cinnamon

⅛ teaspoon nutmeg

2 cups frozen green peas

Slice acorn squash in half, remove seeds and slice each half into 6 slices, approximately ½ inch thick. Place 6 half slices on bottom of 5-quart slow cooker. Arrange 3 pork chops over squash; repeat layers. Combine remaining ingredients except peas; pour over squash mixture. Cover and cook on LOW 5 to 6 hours or until pork and squash are tender. Remove both from slow cooker; keep warm. Stir in frozen peas. Turn heat setting to HIGH. Cover and cook about 5 minutes or until peas are tender; drain.   *Makes 6 servings*

Favorite recipe from **National Pork Board**

Italian Sausage and Peppers

Cook Time: 8¼ to 9¼ hours

3 cups 1-inch bell pepper chunks (preferably a mix of red, yellow and green*)

1 small onion, cut into thin wedges

3 cloves garlic, minced

1 pound hot or mild Italian sausage links

1 cup prepared marinara or pasta sauce

¼ cup red wine or port

1 tablespoon cornstarch

1 tablespoon water

Hot cooked thin spaghetti or chunky pasta

¼ cup grated Parmesan or Romano cheese

Look for mixed bell pepper chunks at your supermarket salad bar. Or substitute 3 small bell peppers (any color or combination) cut into chunks.

1. Coat slow cooker with cooking spray. Place bell peppers, onion and garlic in bottom of slow cooker. Arrange sausage over vegetables. Combine marinara sauce and wine; pour over sausage. Cover and cook on LOW 8 to 9 hours or on HIGH 4 to 5 hours, or until sausage is cooked through and vegetables are tender.

2. Transfer sausage to serving platter; cover with foil to keep warm. Skim off and discard fat from juices in slow cooker. Mix cornstarch with water until smooth; turn heat to HIGH. Cook about 10 minutes or until sauce is thickened, stirring once. Serve sauce over spaghetti and sausage; top with cheese.

Makes 4 servings

Spicy Asian Pork Filling

Prep Time: 15 to 20 minutes   **Cook Time:** 8½ to 10½ hours

1 boneless pork sirloin roast
  (about 3 pounds)

½ cup tamari or other soy sauce

1 tablespoon chili garlic sauce
  or chili paste

2 teaspoons minced fresh ginger

2 tablespoons water

1 tablespoon cornstarch

2 teaspoons dark sesame oil

1. Cut roast into 2- to 3-inch chunks. Combine pork, tamari sauce, chili garlic sauce and ginger in slow cooker; mix well. Cover; cook on LOW 8 to 10 hours or until pork is fork tender.

2. Remove roast from cooking liquid; cool slightly. Trim and discard excess fat. Shred pork using 2 forks. Let liquid stand 5 minutes to allow fat to rise. Skim off fat.

3. Blend water, cornstarch and sesame oil until smooth; stir into slow cooker. Cook, uncovered, on HIGH until thickened. Add shredded meat to slow cooker; mix well. Cover; cook 15 to 30 minutes or until hot.

Makes 5½ cups filling

Spicy Asian Pork Bundles: Place ¼ cup pork filling into large lettuce leaves. Wrap to enclose. Makes about 20 bundles.

Moo Shu Pork: Lightly spread plum sauce over warm small flour tortillas. Spoon ¼ cup pork filling and ¼ cup stir-fried vegetables into flour tortillas. Wrap to enclose. Serve immediately. Makes about 20 wraps.

Pork Roast Landaise

Prep Time: 20 minutes   **Cook Time:** 8 hours

2 tablespoons olive oil

2½ pounds boneless center cut pork loin roast

Salt and pepper

1 medium onion, diced

2 large cloves garlic, minced

2 teaspoons dried thyme

2 parsnips, cut in ¾-inch slices

2 cups chicken stock, divided

2 tablespoons cornstarch

¼ cup red wine vinegar

¼ cup sugar

½ cup port or sherry wine

1½ cups pitted prunes

3 pears, cored and sliced ¾ inch thick

1. Heat olive oil in large saucepan over medium-high heat. Season pork roast with salt and pepper; brown in saucepan on all sides. Place roast in slow cooker.

2. Add onion and garlic to same saucepan. Cook and stir over medium heat 2 to 3 minutes. Stir in thyme. Add onion mixture and parsnips to slow cooker.

3. Combine ¼ cup of chicken stock with cornstarch in small bowl until smooth; set aside.

4. Combine vinegar and sugar in same saucepan. Cook over medium heat, stirring constantly, until mixture thickens into syrup. Add port and cook 1 minute more. Add remaining 1¾ cups chicken stock. Whisk in cornstarch mixture and cook until sauce is smooth and slightly thickened. Pour into slow cooker.

5. Cover; cook on LOW 8 hours or on HIGH 4 hours. During the last 30 minutes of cooking, add prunes and pears. Serve over rice or mashed potatoes or with French bread, if desired.   *Makes 4 to 6 servings*

Cajun-Style Country Ribs

Prep Time: 15 minutes   **Cook Time:** 6¼ to 8¼ hours

2 cups baby carrots

1 large onion, coarsely chopped

1 large green bell pepper, cut into 1-inch pieces

1 large red bell pepper, cut into 1-inch pieces

2 teaspoons minced garlic

2 tablespoons Cajun or Creole seasoning, divided

3½ to 4 pounds pork country-style ribs

1 can (14½ ounces) stewed tomatoes, undrained

2 tablespoons water

1 tablespoon cornstarch

Hot cooked rice

1. Combine carrots, onion, bell peppers, garlic and 2 teaspoons Cajun seasoning in 5-quart slow cooker; mix well.

2. Trim excess fat from ribs. Cut into individual ribs. Sprinkle 1 tablespoon Cajun seasoning over ribs; place in slow cooker over vegetables. Pour tomatoes with juice over ribs. Cover; cook on LOW 6 to 8 hours or until ribs are fork tender.

3. Remove ribs and vegetables from cooking liquid to serving platter. Let liquid stand 5 minutes to allow fat to rise. Skim off fat. Blend water, cornstarch and remaining 1 teaspoon Cajun seasoning until smooth. Stir into slow cooker. Cook, uncovered, on HIGH 15 to 30 minutes or until sauce is thickened. Return ribs and vegetables to sauce; carefully stir to coat. Serve with rice.

Makes 6 to 8 servings

Tasty Poultry

Saucy Tropical Turkey

Prep Time: 15 minutes   **Cook Time:** 6½ to 7½ hours

3 to 4 turkey thighs, skin removed (about 2½ pounds)

2 tablespoons vegetable oil

1 small onion, halved and sliced

1 can (20 ounces) pineapple chunks, drained

1 red bell pepper, cubed

⅔ cup apricot preserves

3 tablespoons soy sauce

1 teaspoon grated lemon peel

1 teaspoon ground ginger

¼ cup cold water

2 tablespoons cornstarch

Hot cooked rice

1. Rinse turkey and pat dry. Heat oil in large skillet; brown turkey on all sides. Place onion in slow cooker. Transfer turkey to slow cooker; top with pineapple and bell pepper.

2. Combine preserves, soy sauce, lemon peel and ginger in small bowl; mix well. Spoon over turkey. Cover; cook on LOW 6 to 7 hours.

3. Remove turkey from slow cooker; keep warm. Blend water and cornstarch until smooth; stir into slow cooker. Cook, uncovered, on HIGH 15 minutes or until sauce is slightly thickened. Adjust seasonings. Return turkey to slow cooker; cook until hot. Serve with rice.

Makes 6 servings

Forty-Clove Chicken

Cook Time: 6 hours

1 frying chicken (3 pounds),
  cut up

Salt and black pepper

1 to 2 tablespoons olive oil

¼ cup dry white wine

2 tablespoons chopped fresh
  parsley *or* 2 teaspoons dried
  parsley flakes

2 tablespoons dry vermouth

2 teaspoons dried basil

1 teaspoon dried oregano

Pinch red pepper flakes

40 cloves garlic (about 2 heads*),
  peeled

4 ribs celery, sliced

Juice and grated peel of
  1 lemon

Fresh parsley

The whole garlic bulb is called a head.

1. Remove skin from chicken. Sprinkle chicken with salt and pepper. Heat oil in large skillet over medium heat. Add chicken; brown on both sides. Remove to platter.

2. Combine wine, parsley, vermouth, basil, oregano and red pepper flakes in large bowl. Add garlic and celery; coat well. Transfer garlic and celery to slow cooker with slotted spoon. Add chicken to remaining herb mixture; coat well. Place chicken on top of celery mixture in slow cooker. Sprinkle lemon juice and peel over chicken; add remaining herb mixture.

3. Cover; cook on LOW 6 hours. Sprinkle with fresh parsley before serving.

Makes 4 to 6 servings

Chicken and Black Bean Chili

1 pound boneless, skinless chicken thighs, cut into 1-inch chunks

2 teaspoons chili powder

2 teaspoons ground cumin

¾ teaspoon salt

1 green bell pepper, diced

1 small onion, chopped

3 cloves garlic, minced

1 can (14½ ounces) diced tomatoes, undrained

1 cup chunky salsa

1 can (16 ounces) black beans, rinsed and drained

Optional toppings: sour cream, diced ripe avocado, shredded Cheddar cheese, sliced green onions or chopped cilantro, crushed tortilla or corn chips

1. Coat slow cooker with cooking spray. Combine chicken, chili powder, cumin and salt in slow cooker, tossing to coat. Add bell pepper, onion and garlic; mix well. Stir in tomatoes with juice and salsa. Cover and cook on LOW 5 to 6 hours or on HIGH 2½ to 3 hours, or until chicken is tender.

2. Turn heat to HIGH; stir in beans. Cover and cook 10 to 15 minutes or until beans are heated through. Ladle into shallow bowls; serve with desired toppings. *Makes 4 servings*

Coq au Vin

Cook Time: $6\frac{1}{4}$ to $8\frac{1}{4}$ hours

2 cups frozen pearl onions, thawed

4 slices bacon, crisp-cooked and crumbled

1 cup sliced button mushrooms

1 clove garlic, minced

1 teaspoon dried thyme

$\frac{1}{8}$ teaspoon black pepper

6 boneless skinless chicken breasts (about 2 pounds)

$\frac{1}{2}$ cup dry red wine

$\frac{3}{4}$ cup reduced-sodium chicken broth

$\frac{1}{4}$ cup tomato paste

3 tablespoons all-purpose flour

Hot cooked egg noodles (optional)

1. Layer onions, bacon, mushrooms, garlic, thyme, pepper, chicken, wine and broth in slow cooker.

2. Cover; cook on LOW 6 to 8 hours.

3. Remove chicken and vegetables; cover and keep warm. Ladle $\frac{1}{2}$ cup cooking liquid into small bowl; cool slightly. Whisk reserved liquid, tomato paste and flour until smooth; stir into slow cooker. Cook; uncovered, on HIGH 15 minutes or until thickened. Serve over hot noodles, if desired.

Makes 6 servings

Herbed Turkey Breast with Orange Sauce

Cook Time: 7 to 8 hours

1 large onion, chopped

3 cloves garlic, minced

1 teaspoon dried rosemary

½ teaspoon black pepper

1 boneless skinless turkey breast (2 to 3 pounds)

1½ cups orange juice

1. Place onion in slow cooker. Combine garlic, rosemary and pepper in small bowl; set aside. Cut slices about three fourths of the way through turkey at 2-inch intervals. Rub garlic mixture between slices.

2. Place turkey, cut side up, in slow cooker. Pour orange juice over turkey. Cover; cook on LOW 7 to 8 hours.

3. Serve sauce from slow cooker with sliced turkey. *Makes 4 to 6 servings*

Southwestern-Style Chicken

Prep Time: 20 minutes   **Cook Time:** 6 to 7 hours

1 package (about 1¼ ounces) taco seasoning mix

¼ cup all-purpose flour

6 to 8 boneless skinless chicken thighs or breasts

2 tablespoons vegetable oil

1 large onion, cut into 1-inch pieces

2 green bell peppers, cut into 1-inch pieces

1 can (14½ ounces) diced tomatoes with jalapeños, undrained

Salt and black pepper

1. Reserve 1 teaspoon taco seasoning. Combine flour and remaining seasoning in plastic food storage bag. Add chicken, 1 to 2 pieces at a time; shake to coat.

2. Heat oil in large skillet over medium-high heat; brown chicken. Transfer chicken to slow cooker; sprinkle with reserved seasoning.

3. Add onion to skillet; cook and stir until translucent. Transfer onion to slow cooker. Add green peppers and tomatoes with juice. Cover; cook on LOW 6 to 7 hours or until chicken is tender. Season with salt and black pepper. *Makes 4 to 6 servings*

Three-Bean Turkey Chili

Cook Time: 6 to 8 hours

1 pound ground turkey

1 small onion, chopped

1 can (28 ounces) diced
   tomatoes, undrained

1 can (15 ounces) chick-peas,
   rinsed and drained

1 can (15 ounces) kidney beans,
   rinsed and drained

1 can (15 ounces) black beans,
   rinsed and drained

1 can (8 ounces) tomato sauce

1 can (about 4 ounces) chopped
   mild green chilies

1 to 2 tablespoons chili powder

1. Cook turkey and onion in medium skillet over medium-high heat until turkey is no longer pink, stirring to break up meat. Drain; place turkey mixture into slow cooker.

2. Add remaining ingredients and mix well. Cover; cook on LOW 6 to 8 hours.

Makes 6 to 8 servings

Sensational Sides

Cheesy Broccoli Casserole

Prep Time: 5 to 10 minutes   **Cook Time:** 5½ to 7 hours

2 packages (10 ounces each)
   chopped broccoli

1 can (10¾ ounces) condensed
   cream of potato soup

1¼ cups (5 ounces) shredded
   sharp Cheddar cheese,
   divided

¼ cup minced onion

1 teaspoon hot pepper sauce

1 cup crushed saltine crackers
   or potato chips

1. Lightly grease slow cooker. Combine broccoli, soup, 1 cup cheese, onion and pepper sauce in slow cooker; mix well.

2. Cover; cook on LOW 5 to 6 hours or on HIGH 2½ to 3 hours.

3. Sprinkle crackers and remaining ½ cup cheese over broccoli mixture. Cook, uncovered, on LOW 30 to 60 minutes or until cheese melts.   *Makes 4 to 6 servings*

Note: For a crispy topping, transfer casserole to a baking dish. Sprinkle with remaining cheese and crackers. Bake 10 to 15 minutes in preheated 400°F oven.

Winter Squash and Apples

Prep Time: 15 minutes   **Cook Time:** 6 to 7 hours

1 teaspoon salt

½ teaspoon black pepper

1 butternut squash (about 2 pounds), peeled and seeded

2 apples, cored and cut into slices

1 medium onion, quartered and sliced

1½ tablespoons butter

1. Combine salt and pepper in small bowl; set aside.

2. Cut squash into 2-inch pieces; place in slow cooker. Add apples and onion. Sprinkle with salt mixture; stir well. Cover; cook on LOW 6 to 7 hours.

3. Just before serving, stir in butter and season with additional salt and pepper.

Makes 4 to 6 servings

Variation: Add ¼ to ½ cup packed brown sugar and ½ teaspoon ground cinnamon with butter; mix well.

Rustic Potatoes au Gratin

Cook Time: 6½ to 7 hours

½ cup milk

1 can (10¾ ounces) condensed Cheddar cheese soup, undiluted

1 package (8 ounces) cream cheese, softened

1 clove garlic, minced

¼ teaspoon ground nutmeg

⅛ teaspoon black pepper

2 pounds baking potatoes, cut into ¼-inch slices

1 small onion, thinly sliced

Paprika (optional)

1. Heat milk in small saucepan over medium heat until small bubbles form around edge of pan. Remove from heat. Add soup, cream cheese, garlic, nutmeg and pepper. Stir until smooth.

2. Layer ¼ of potatoes and ¼ of onion in bottom of slow cooker. Top with ¼ of soup mixture. Repeat layers 3 times, using remaining potatoes, onion and soup mixture.

3. Cover; cook on LOW 6½ to 7 hours or until potatoes are tender and most of liquid is absorbed. Sprinkle with paprika, if desired.

Makes 6 servings

Bean Pot Medley

1 can (15½ ounces) black beans, rinsed and drained

1 can (15½ ounces) red beans, rinsed and drained

1 can (15½ ounces) Great Northern beans, rinsed and drained

1 can (15½ ounces) black-eyed peas, rinsed and drained

1 can (8½ ounces) baby lima beans, rinsed and drained

1½ cups ketchup

1 cup chopped onion

1 cup chopped red bell pepper

1 cup chopped green bell pepper

½ cup packed brown sugar

½ cup water

2 to 3 teaspoons cider vinegar

1 teaspoon dry mustard

2 bay leaves

⅛ teaspoon black pepper

1. Combine beans, peas, ketchup, onion, bell peppers, brown sugar, water, vinegar, mustard, bay leaves and black pepper in 4-quart slow cooker; mix well.

2. Cover; cook on LOW 6 to 7 hours or until onion and bell peppers are tender.

3. Remove and discard bay leaves before serving.

Makes 8 servings

Red Cabbage and Apples

Cook Time: 6 hours (HIGH)

1 small head red cabbage, cored and thinly sliced

3 medium apples, peeled and grated

¾ cup sugar

½ cup red wine vinegar

1 teaspoon ground cloves

1 cup crisp-cooked and crumbled bacon (optional)

Combine cabbage, apples, sugar, vinegar and cloves in slow cooker. Cover; cook on HIGH 6 hours, stirring after 3 hours. Sprinkle with bacon, if desired. Garnish as desired.

Makes 4 to 6 servings

Scalloped Potatoes and Parsnips

Cook Time: 7 hours

6 tablespoons unsalted butter

3 tablespoons all-purpose flour

1¾ cups whipping cream

2 teaspoons dry mustard

1½ teaspoons salt

1 teaspoon dried thyme

½ teaspoon black pepper

2 baking potatoes, cut in half lengthwise, then crosswise into ¼ inch slices

2 parsnips, cut into ¼-inch slices

1 onion, chopped

2 cups (8 ounces) shredded sharp Cheddar cheese

1. Melt butter in medium saucepan over medium-high heat. Add flour and whisk constantly 1 to 2 minutes. Slowly whisk in cream, mustard, salt, thyme and pepper. Stir until mixture comes to a boil.

2. Place potatoes, parsnips and onion in slow cooker. Add cream sauce.

3. Cover; cook on LOW 7 hours or on HIGH 3½ hours or until potatoes are tender. Stir in cheese. Cover; let stand until cheese melts.

Makes 4 to 6 servings

Spanish Paella-Style Rice

Prep Time: 10 minutes   **Cook Time:** 4½ hours

2 cans (14½ ounces each) chicken broth

1½ cups uncooked converted long grain rice

1 small red bell pepper, diced

⅓ cup dry white wine or water

½ teaspoon powdered saffron *or* ½ teaspoon ground turmeric

⅛ teaspoon red pepper flakes

½ cup frozen peas, thawed

Salt

1. Combine broth, rice, bell pepper, wine, saffron and pepper flakes in 2½-quart slow cooker; mix well.

2. Cover; cook on LOW 4 hours or until liquid is absorbed.

3. Stir in peas. Cover; cook 15 to 30 minutes or until peas are hot. Season with salt.

Makes 6 servings

Note: Since saffron is very expensive, turmeric is given as an alternative; with turmeric the finished dish will look similar but the flavor will differ.

Variations: Add ½ cup shredded cooked chicken or ham, shrimp or quartered marinated artichokes, drained, with peas.

Orange-Spiced Sweet Potatoes

Cook Time: 4 hours

2 pounds sweet potatoes, peeled and diced

½ cup dark brown sugar, packed

½ cup butter (1 stick), cut into small pieces

1 teaspoon ground cinnamon

½ teaspoon ground nutmeg

½ teaspoon grated orange peel

Juice of 1 medium orange

¼ teaspoon salt

1 teaspoon vanilla

Chopped toasted pecans (optional)

Place sweet potatoes, brown sugar, butter, cinnamon, nutmeg, orange peel, orange juice, salt and vanilla in slow cooker. Cover and cook on LOW 4 hours or on HIGH 2 hours or until potatoes are tender. Sprinkle with pecans before serving, if desired.

Makes 8 servings

Variation: Mash potatoes with a hand masher or electric mixer; add ¼ cup milk or whipping cream for a moister consistency. Sprinkle with a mixture of sugar and ground cinnamon.

Sweet Potato & Pecan Casserole

Cook Time: 3 to 4 hours (HIGH)

1 can (40 ounces) sweet potatoes, drained and mashed

½ cup apple juice

⅓ cup plus 2 tablespoons butter, melted, divided

½ teaspoon salt

½ teaspoon ground cinnamon

¼ teaspoon black pepper

2 eggs, beaten

⅓ cup chopped pecans

⅓ cup brown sugar

2 tablespoons all-purpose flour

1. Lightly grease slow cooker. Combine sweet potatoes, apple juice, ⅓ cup butter, salt, cinnamon and pepper in large bowl. Stir in eggs. Place mixture into prepared slow cooker.

2. Combine pecans, brown sugar, flour and remaining 2 tablespoons butter in small bowl. Spread over sweet potatoes.

3. Cover; cook on HIGH 3 to 4 hours.

Makes 6 to 8 servings

Tip: This casserole is excellent to make for the holidays. Using the slow cooker frees the oven for other dishes.

Scalloped Tomatoes & Corn

Prep Time: 7 minutes   **Cook Time:** 4 to 6 hours

1 can (15 ounces) cream-style corn

1 can (14½ ounces) diced tomatoes, undrained

¾ cup saltine cracker crumbs

1 egg, lightly beaten

2 teaspoons sugar

¾ teaspoon black pepper

Combine corn, tomatoes with juice, cracker crumbs, egg, sugar and pepper in slow cooker; mix well. Cover; cook on LOW 4 to 6 hours.

Makes 4 to 6 servings

Spinach Spoonbread

Cook Time: 3 to 4 hours

1 package (10 ounces) frozen chopped spinach, thawed and squeezed dry

1 red bell pepper, diced

4 eggs, lightly beaten

1 cup cottage cheese

1 package (5½ ounces) cornbread mix

6 green onions, sliced

½ cup (1 stick) butter, melted

1¼ teaspoons seasoned salt

1. Lightly grease slow cooker; preheat on HIGH.

2. Combine all ingredients in large bowl; mix well. Pour batter into preheated slow cooker. Cook, covered with lid slightly ajar to allow excess moisture to escape, on LOW 3 to 4 hours or on HIGH 1¾ to 2 hours or until edges are golden and knife inserted in center of bread comes out clean.

3. Serve bread spooned from slow cooker, or loosen edges and bottom with knife and invert onto plate. Cut into wedges to serve.

Makes 8 servings

Green Bean Casserole

Cook Time: 3 to 4 hours

2 packages (10 ounces each) frozen green beans, thawed

1 can (10½ ounces) condensed cream of mushroom soup

1 tablespoon chopped fresh parsley

1 tablespoon chopped roasted red peppers

1 teaspoon dried sage

½ teaspoon salt

½ teaspoon black pepper

¼ teaspoon ground nutmeg

½ cup toasted slivered almonds

1. Combine green beans, soup, parsley, roasted red peppers, sage, salt, black pepper and nutmeg in slow cooker.

2. Cover; cook on LOW 3 to 4 hours. Sprinkle with almonds.

Makes 4 to 6 servings

Escalloped Corn

Cook Time: 3 ½ to 4 hours

2 tablespoons butter

½ cup chopped onion

3 tablespoons all-purpose flour

1 cup milk

4 cups frozen corn, thawed, divided

½ teaspoon salt

½ teaspoon dried thyme

¼ teaspoon black pepper

⅛ teaspoon ground nutmeg

Fresh thyme (optional)

1. Melt butter in small saucepan over medium heat. Add onion; cook and stir 5 minutes or until tender. Add flour. Cook over medium heat 1 minute, stirring constantly. Stir in milk; bring to a boil. Boil 1 minute or until thickened, stirring constantly.

2. Process 2 cups corn in food processor or blender until coarsely chopped. Combine milk mixture, chopped and whole corn, salt, dried thyme, pepper and nutmeg in slow cooker; mix well.

3. Cover; cook on LOW 3 ½ to 4 hours or until mixture is bubbly around edge. Garnish with fresh thyme, if desired.   *Makes 6 servings*

Variation: Add ½ cup (2 ounces) shredded Cheddar cheese and 2 tablespoons grated Parmesan cheese before serving; stir until melted. Garnish with additional shredded Cheddar cheese.

BEST SLOW-COOKER

R E C I P E S

Contents

Simmering Soups

Peppery Potato Soup

Prep Time: 15 minutes   **Cook Time:** 7½ to 9 hours

2 cans (14½ ounces each)
   chicken broth

4 small baking potatoes, halved
   and sliced

1 large onion, quartered and
   sliced crosswise

1 rib celery, sliced

½ teaspoon salt

½ teaspoon black pepper

1 cup half-and-half

¼ cup all-purpose flour

1 tablespoon butter

   Celery leaves and fresh parsley
   (optional)

1. Combine broth, potatoes, onion, celery, salt and pepper in slow cooker; mix well. Cover; cook on LOW 6 to 7½ hours.

2. Whisk half-and-half into flour; stir mixture into slow cooker. Cover; cook 1 hour.

3. Slightly mash potato mixture with potato masher. Cook, uncovered, 30 minutes or until slightly thickened. Just before serving, stir in butter. Garnish with celery leaves and parsley, if desired. *Makes 6 servings*

Mediterranean Shrimp Soup

Cook Time: 4½ hours

2 cans (14½ ounces each)
   reduced-sodium chicken
   broth

1 can (about 14½ ounces) diced
   tomatoes, undrained

1 can (8 ounces) tomato sauce

1 medium onion, chopped

½ medium green bell pepper,
   chopped

½ cup orange juice

½ cup dry white wine (optional)

1 jar (4 ounces) sliced
   mushrooms

¼ cup ripe olives, sliced

2 cloves garlic, minced

1 teaspoon dried basil

2 bay leaves

¼ teaspoon fennel seeds,
   crushed

⅛ teaspoon black pepper

1 pound uncooked medium
   shrimp, peeled

1. Combine broth, tomatoes with juice, tomato sauce, onion, bell pepper, juice, wine, if desired, mushrooms, olives, garlic, basil, bay leaves, fennel seeds and black pepper in slow cooker. Cover; cook on LOW 4 to 4½ hours or until vegetables are tender.

2. Turn slow cooker to HIGH. Stir in shrimp. Cover; cook 15 to 30 minutes or until shrimp are opaque. Remove and discard bay leaves.

Makes 6 servings

Note: For a heartier soup, add some fish. Cut 1 pound of whitefish or cod into 1-inch pieces. Add the fish to the slow cooker 45 minutes before serving. Cover and cook on LOW.

Butternut Squash-Apple Soup

Cook Time: 6 hours

3 packages (12 ounces each) frozen cooked winter squash, thawed and drained *or* 4½ cups mashed cooked butternut squash

2 cans (14½ ounces each) chicken broth

1 medium Golden Delicious apple, peeled, cored and chopped

2 tablespoons minced onion

1 tablespoon packed brown sugar

1 teaspoon minced fresh sage *or* ½ teaspoon ground sage

¼ teaspoon ground ginger

½ cup whipping cream

1. Combine squash, broth, apple, onion, brown sugar, sage and ginger in slow cooker.

2. Cover; cook on LOW about 6 hours or on HIGH about 3 hours or until squash is tender.

3. Purée soup in blender or food processor. Stir in cream just before serving.

Makes 6 to 8 servings

Tip: For thicker soup, use only 3 cups chicken broth.

Tuscan White Bean Soup

Cook Time: 8 hours

6 ounces bacon, diced

10 cups chicken broth

1 bag (16 ounces) dried Great Northern beans, rinsed

1 can (14½ ounces) diced tomatoes, undrained

1 large onion, chopped

3 carrots, chopped

4 cloves garlic, minced

1 fresh rosemary sprig *or* 1 teaspoon dried rosemary

1 teaspoon black pepper

1. Cook bacon in medium skillet over medium-high heat until crisp; drain and transfer to 5-quart slow cooker. Add remaining ingredients.

2. Cover; cook on LOW 8 hours or until vegetables are tender. Remove and discard rosemary sprig before serving.

Makes 8 to 10 servings

Serving Suggestion: Place slices of toasted Italian bread in bottom of individual soup bowls. Drizzle with olive oil. Pour soup over bread and serve.

Red Bean Soup with Andouille Sausage

Cook Time: 4½ hours

2 tablespoons unsalted butter

1 large sweet onion, diced

3 stalks celery, diced

2 large cloves garlic, chopped

8 cups chicken broth

1 ham hock

1½ cups dried red kidney beans, soaked in cold water 1 hour, rinsed and drained

1 bay leaf

2 parsnips, diced

1 sweet potato, peeled and diced

1 pound andouille sausage or kielbasa, cut into ½-inch pieces

Salt and black pepper

1. Melt butter in large saucepan over medium heat. Cook and stir onion, celery and garlic 5 minutes. Place in 6-quart slow cooker. Add broth, ham hock, kidney beans and bay leaf. Cover; cook on HIGH 2 hours.

2. Remove ham hock; discard. Add parsnips and sweet potato. Cover; cook 2 hours.

3. Add sausage. Cover; cook 30 minutes or until heated through. Remove and discard bay leaf. Season with salt and pepper.

Makes 6 to 8 servings

Note: Use a 6-quart slow cooker for this recipe. If using a smaller slow cooker, cut all ingredients in half.

Simmered Split Pea Soup

Prep Time: 15 minutes   **Cook Time:** 6 to 8 hours

3 cans (14½ ounces each) chicken broth

1 package (16 ounces) split peas

1 medium onion, diced

2 medium carrots, diced

1 teaspoon black pepper

½ teaspoon dried thyme

1 bay leaf

8 slices bacon, crisp-cooked and crumbled, divided

1. Place broth, split peas, onion, carrots, pepper, thyme, bay leaf and half of bacon in slow cooker. Cover; cook on LOW 6 to 8 hours or until vegetables are tender.

2. Remove and discard bay leaf. Adjust seasonings, if desired. Garnish with remaining bacon.

Makes 6 servings

Sausage, Butter Bean and Cabbage Soup

Cook Time: 5 hours

2 tablespoons butter, divided

1 large onion, chopped

12 ounces smoked sausage such as kielbasa or andouille, cut into ½-inch slices

8 cups chicken broth

½ savoy cabbage, coarsely shredded

3 tablespoons tomato paste

1 bay leaf

4 medium tomatoes, chopped

2 cans (14 ounces each) butter beans, drained

Salt and black pepper

1. Melt 1 tablespoon butter in large skillet over medium heat. Add onion; cook and stir 3 to 4 minutes or until golden. Place in slow cooker.

2. Melt remaining 1 tablespoon butter in same skillet; cook sausage until brown. Add to slow cooker.

3. Place chicken broth, cabbage, tomato paste and bay leaf in slow cooker; stir until well blended. Cover; cook on LOW 4 hours or HIGH 2 hours.

4. Add tomatoes and beans; season with salt and pepper. Cover; cook 1 hour until heated through. Remove and discard bay leaf.

Makes 6 servings

Tip: Savoy cabbage is an excellent cooking cabbage with a full head of crinkled leaves varying from dark to pale green. Green cabbage may be substituted.

Italian Beef and Barley Soup

Prep Time: 20 minutes   **Cook Time:** 8 to 10 hours

1 boneless beef top sirloin steak (about 1½ pounds)

1 tablespoon vegetable oil

4 medium carrots or parsnips, cut into ¼-inch slices

1 cup chopped onion

1 teaspoon dried thyme

½ teaspoon dried rosemary

¼ teaspoon black pepper

⅓ cup pearl barley

2 cans (14½ ounces each) beef broth

1 can (14½ ounces) diced tomatoes with Italian seasoning, undrained

1. Cut beef into 1-inch pieces. Heat oil over medium-high heat in large skillet. Brown beef on all sides; set aside.

2. Place carrots and onion in slow cooker; sprinkle with thyme, rosemary and pepper. Top with barley and meat. Pour broth and tomatoes with juice over meat.

3. Cover; cook on LOW 8 to 10 hours or until beef is tender.   *Makes 6 servings*

Lamb Meatball & Chick-Pea Soup

Cook Time: 4 to 5 hours

1 pound ground lamb

¼ cup chopped onion

1 clove garlic, minced

1 teaspoon ground cumin

½ teaspoon salt

2 cups chicken broth

1 (15-ounce) can diced tomatoes, drained

1 (15-ounce) can chick-peas, drained

1 (10-ounce) package frozen chopped broccoli, thawed

½ teaspoon dried thyme

Salt and black pepper

1. Combine lamb, onion, garlic, cumin and salt; mix lightly. Shape into 1-inch balls.* Brown meatballs in large skillet over medium-high heat, turning occasionally.

2. Place broth, tomatoes, chick-peas, broccoli, thyme and meatballs in slow cooker. Cover; cook on LOW 4 to 5 hours. Season to taste with salt and black pepper.

Makes 4 to 6 servings

To quickly shape uniform meatballs, place meat mixture on cutting board; pat evenly into large square, 1 inch thick. With sharp knife, cut meat into 1-inch squares; shape each square into a ball.

Beef, Pork & Lamb

Sweet and Sour Spareribs

Cook Time: 6¼ hours

4 pounds pork spareribs

1⅓ cup chicken broth

1 cup dry sherry or chicken broth

½ cup pineapple, mango or guava juice

2 tablespoons packed brown sugar

2 tablespoons cider vinegar

2 tablespoons soy sauce

1 clove garlic, minced

½ teaspoon salt

¼ teaspoon black pepper

⅛ teaspoon red pepper flakes

2 tablespoons cornstarch

¼ cup water

1. Preheat oven to 400°F. Place ribs in foil-lined shallow roasting pan. Bake 30 minutes, turning over after 15 minutes. Remove from oven. Slice meat into 2-rib portions. Place ribs in 5-quart slow cooker. Add remaining ingredients, except cornstarch and water, to slow cooker.

2. Cover; cook on LOW 6 hours or until ribs are tender. Transfer ribs to platter; keep warm. Let liquid in slow cooker stand 5 minutes to allow fat to rise. Skim off fat.

3. Blend cornstarch and water until smooth. Stir mixture into slow cooker; mix well. Cook, uncovered, on HIGH 15 minutes or until slightly thickened. *Makes 4 servings*

Mexican-Style Shredded Beef

Prep Time: 12 minutes   **Cook Time:** 8½ to 10½ hours

1 boneless beef chuck shoulder
　roast (about 3 pounds)
1 tablespoon ground cumin
1 tablespoon ground coriander
1 tablespoon chili powder
1 teaspoon salt
½ teaspoon ground red pepper
1 cup salsa or picante sauce
2 tablespoons water
1 tablespoon cornstarch
　Taco shells

1. Cut roast in half. Combine cumin, coriander, chili powder, salt and red pepper in small bowl. Rub over beef. Place ¼ cup salsa in slow cooker; top with one piece beef. Layer ¼ cup salsa, remaining piece of beef and ½ cup salsa in slow cooker. Cover; cook on LOW 8 to 10 hours or until meat is tender.

2. Remove beef from cooking liquid; cool slightly. Trim and discard excess fat from beef. Shred meat with two forks.

3. Let cooking liquid stand 5 minutes to allow fat to rise. Skim off fat. Blend water and cornstarch until smooth. Whisk into liquid in slow cooker. Cook, uncovered, 15 minutes on HIGH until thickened. Return beef to slow cooker. Cover; cook 15 minutes or until hot. Adjust seasonings, if desired. Serve as meat filling for tacos, fajitas or burritos. Leftover beef may be refrigerated up to 3 days or frozen up to 3 months.

Makes 5 cups filling

Beef Stew with Bacon, Onion & Sweet Potatoes

Cook Time: 7¼ to 8¼ hours

1 pound lean beef stew meat
    (1-inch chunks)

1 can (14½ ounces) beef broth

2 medium sweet potatoes,
    peeled, cut into 2-inch
    chunks*

1 large onion, cut into 1½-inch
    chunks

2 slices thick-cut bacon, diced

1 teaspoon dried thyme

1 teaspoon salt

¼ teaspoon black pepper

2 tablespoons cornstarch

2 tablespoons water

*You may substitute 12 ounces of
carrots or white potatoes, cut into
2-inch chunks for the sweet potatoes.*

1. Coat slow cooker with cooking spray. Combine all ingredients except cornstarch and water in slow cooker; mix well. Cover; cook on LOW 7 to 8 hours or on HIGH 4 to 5 hours or until meat and vegetables are tender.

2. With slotted spoon, transfer beef and vegetables to serving bowl; cover with foil to keep warm. Turn slow cooker to HIGH. Combine cornstarch with water until smooth. Stir into juices; cover and cook 15 minutes or until thickened. Spoon sauce over beef and vegetables. *Makes 4 servings*

Lamb Stew

Cook Time: 7½ hours

1 large onion, chopped

2½ to 3½ tablespoons olive oil, divided

½ cup all-purpose flour

2 teaspoons salt

1 teaspoon black pepper

3 pounds boneless lamb for stew, cut into 2- to 2½-inch pieces

2 tablespoons sugar, divided

3 cans (14½ ounces each) beef broth

3 tablespoons tomato paste

4 cloves garlic, chopped

1 tablespoon dried thyme

1 tablespoon fresh chopped rosemary

2 bay leaves

1 pound carrots, cut into 2-inch chunks

1 pound petite Yukon gold potatoes, peeled and cut into halves

1 package (10 ounces) frozen peas, thawed

1. Cook and stir onion in ½ tablespoon olive oil in large skillet over medium heat until golden. Add to 4- to 5-quart slow cooker.

2. Combine flour, salt and pepper in large bowl. Dredge lamb in flour mixture. Heat 1 tablespoon oil in skillet over medium-high heat until hot. Add half of lamb; cook until browned on all sides. Add 1 tablespoon sugar; mix well to coat meat. Cook 3 to 4 minutes or until meat is caramelized. Add meat to slow cooker. Repeat with remaining lamb, using remaining 1 to 2 tablespoons oil as needed and remaining 1 tablespoon sugar.

3. Add broth to skillet; bring to a boil over high heat, scraping sides and bottom of pan to loosen browned bits. Add tomato paste, garlic, thyme, rosemary and bay leaves. Mix well. Pour over meat mixture. Cover; cook on LOW 4 hours or on HIGH 2 hours.

4. Add carrots and potatoes. Cover; cook on LOW 3 to 4 hours or on HIGH 1½ to 2½ hours or until vegetables and lamb are tender.

5. Add peas. Cook 30 minutes. Remove and discard bay leaves before serving.

Makes 6 to 8 servings

Curry Beef

Cook Time: 4½ hours

1 pound 90% lean ground beef

1 medium onion, thinly sliced

½ cup beef broth

1 tablespoon curry powder

1 teaspoon ground cumin

2 cloves garlic, minced

1 cup (8 ounces) sour cream

¼ cup milk

½ cup raisins, divided

1 teaspoon sugar

12 ounces wide egg noodles *or* 1⅓ cups long-grain white rice

¼ cup chopped walnuts, almonds or pecans

1. Brown beef in large skillet over medium-high heat, stirring to break up meat. Drain fat.

2. Add onion, beef broth, curry powder, cumin, garlic and beef to slow cooker. Cover; cook on LOW 4 hours. Stir in sour cream, milk, ¼ cup raisins and sugar. Cover; cook 30 minutes or until thickened and heated through.

3. Meanwhile, cook noodles according to package directions; drain. Spoon beef curry over noodles. Sprinkle with remaining ¼ cup raisins and walnuts. *Makes 4 servings*

Serving Suggestion: Serve with sliced cucumber sprinkled with sugar and vinegar or plain yogurt topped with brown sugar, chopped bananas and green onions.

Slow Cooker Steak Fajitas

Prep Time: 20 minutes   **Cook Time:** 6 to 7 hours

1 beef flank steak (about 1 pound)

1 medium onion, cut into strips

½ cup medium salsa

2 tablespoons chopped fresh cilantro

2 tablespoons fresh lime juice

2 cloves garlic, minced

1 tablespoon chili powder

1 teaspoon ground cumin

½ teaspoon salt

1 small green bell pepper, cut into strips

1 small red bell pepper, cut into strips

Flour tortillas, warmed

Additional salsa

1. Cut flank steak lengthwise in half, then crosswise into thin strips; place in slow cooker. Combine onion, ½ cup salsa, cilantro, lime juice, garlic, chili powder, cumin and salt; add to slow cooker.

2. Cover; cook on LOW 5 to 6 hours. Add bell peppers. Cover; cook on LOW 1 hour.

3. Serve with flour tortillas and additional salsa.

Makes 4 servings

Best-Ever Barbecued Ribs

Cook Time: 7½ to 8½ hours

1 teaspoon paprika or smoked paprika

1 teaspoon salt

1 teaspoon dried thyme

¼ teaspoon black pepper

⅛ teaspoon ground red pepper

3 to 3½ pounds well trimmed pork baby back ribs, cut into 4-rib pieces

¼ cup ketchup

2 tablespoons brown sugar

1 tablespoon Worcestershire sauce

1 tablespoon soy sauce

1. Coat slow cooker with cooking spray. Combine paprika, salt, thyme and peppers; rub onto meaty sides of ribs. Place ribs in 3½-quart slow cooker. Cover and cook on LOW 7 to 8 hours or on HIGH 3 to 3½ hours or until ribs are tender.

2. Combine ketchup, brown sugar, Worcestershire sauce and soy sauce; mix well. Remove ribs from slow cooker; discard liquid. Turn slow cooker to HIGH. Coat ribs with sauce. Return to slow cooker; cook 30 minutes or until ribs are glazed.

Makes 6 servings

Rio Grande Ribs

Prep Time: 10 minutes   **Cook Time:** about 6 hours

3 pounds country-style pork ribs, trimmed of all visible fat

1 cup picante sauce

¼ cup beer, non-alcoholic malt beverage or beef broth

1 tablespoon *French's®* Bold n' Spicy Brown Mustard

1 tablespoon *French's®* Worcestershire Sauce

1 teaspoon chili powder

2 tablespoons cornstarch

2 tablespoons water

2 cups *French's®* French Fried Onions, divided

1. Place ribs in slow cooker. Combine picante sauce, beer, mustard, Worcestershire and chili powder in small bowl. Pour mixture over ribs.

2. Cover and cook on LOW setting for 6 hours (or on HIGH for 3 hours) until ribs are tender. Transfer ribs to serving platter; keep warm. Skim fat from sauce.

3. Turn slow cooker to HIGH. Combine cornstarch and water in small bowl; stir into sauce in slow cooker. Add *1 cup* French Fried Onions. Cook 10 to 15 minutes or until thickened. Spoon sauce over ribs; sprinkle with remaining onions. *Makes 4 to 6 servings*

Italian-Style Pot Roast

Prep Time: 15 minutes   **Cook Time:** 8¼ to 9¼ hours

2 teaspoons minced garlic

1 teaspoon salt

1 teaspoon dried basil

1 teaspoon dried oregano

¼ teaspoon red pepper flakes

1 boneless beef bottom round rump or chuck shoulder roast (about 2½ to 3 pounds)

1 large onion, quartered and thinly sliced

1½ cups prepared tomato-basil or marinara pasta sauce

2 cans (15 ounces each) cannellini or Great Northern beans, drained

¼ cup shredded fresh basil or chopped Italian parsley

1. Combine garlic, salt, basil, oregano and pepper flakes in small bowl; rub over roast.

2. Place half of onion slices into 3-quart slow cooker. Cut roast in half to fit into slow cooker. Place one half of roast over onion slices; top with remaining onion slices and other half of roast. Pour pasta sauce over roast. Cover; cook on LOW 8 to 9 hours or until roast is fork tender.

3. Remove roast from cooking liquid; tent with foil. Let liquid in slow cooker stand 5 minutes to allow fat to rise. Skim off fat.

4. Stir beans into liquid. Cover; cook on HIGH 15 to 30 minutes or until beans are hot. Carve roast across the grain into thin slices. Serve with bean mixture and sprinkle with fresh basil.

Makes 6 to 8 servings

Slow-Cooked Korean Beef Short Ribs

Prep Time: 10 to 15 minutes   **Cook Time:** $7\frac{1}{4}$ to $8\frac{1}{4}$ hours

4 to 4½ pounds beef short ribs

¼ cup chopped green onions with tops

¼ cup tamari or soy sauce

¼ cup beef broth or water

1 tablespoon brown sugar

2 teaspoons minced fresh ginger

2 teaspoons minced garlic

½ teaspoon black pepper

2 teaspoons dark sesame oil

Hot cooked rice or linguini pasta

2 teaspoons sesame seeds, toasted

1. Place ribs in 5-quart slow cooker. Combine green onions, tamari, broth, brown sugar, ginger, garlic and pepper in medium bowl; mix well and pour over ribs. Cover; cook on LOW 7 to 8 hours or until ribs are fork tender.

2. Remove ribs from cooking liquid. Cool slightly. Trim excess fat. Cut rib meat into bite-size pieces, discarding bones and fat.

3. Let cooking liquid stand 5 minutes to allow fat to rise. Skim off fat.

4. Stir sesame oil into liquid. Return rib meat to slow cooker. Cover; cook 15 to 30 minutes or until hot.

5. Serve with rice; garnish with sesame seeds.   *Makes 6 servings*

Variation: Three pounds boneless short ribs can be substituted for beef short ribs.

Pork Chops with Jalapeño-Pecan Cornbread Stuffing

Cook Time: 5 hours

6 boneless loin pork chops,
 1 inch thick (1½ pounds)

Nonstick cooking spray

¾ cup chopped onion

¾ cup chopped celery

½ cup coarsely chopped pecans

½ medium jalapeño pepper,*
 seeded and chopped

1 teaspoon rubbed sage

½ teaspoon dried rosemary

⅛ teaspoon black pepper

4 cups unseasoned cornbread
 stuffing mix

1¼ cups reduced-sodium chicken
 broth

1 egg, lightly beaten

*Jalapeño peppers can sting and irritate
the skin; wear rubber gloves when
handling peppers and do not touch
eyes. Wash hands after handling.

1. Trim excess fat from pork. Spray large skillet with nonstick cooking spray; heat over medium heat. Add pork; cook 10 minutes or until browned on both sides. Remove; set aside. Add onion, celery, pecans, jalapeño pepper, sage, rosemary and black pepper to skillet. Cook 5 minutes or until onion and celery are tender; set aside.

2. Combine cornbread stuffing mix, vegetable mixture and broth in medium bowl. Stir in egg. Spoon stuffing mixture into slow cooker. Arrange pork on top. Cover and cook on LOW about 5 hours or until pork is tender and barely pink in center. Serve with vegetable salad, if desired.   *Makes 6 servings*

Note: If you prefer a more moist dressing, increase the chicken broth to 1½ cups.

Chicken & Turkey

San Marino Chicken

Prep Time: 5 minutes   **Cook Time:** 6 hours

1 chicken (3 pounds), skinned and cut up

¼ cup all-purpose flour

1 can (8 ounces) tomato sauce

⅓ cup chopped sun-dried tomatoes packed in oil

¼ cup red wine

1 tablespoon grated lemon peel

2 cups sliced mushrooms

2 cups *French's*® French Fried Onions, divided

Hot cooked rice or pasta (optional)

1. Lightly coat chicken pieces with flour. Place chicken in slow cooker. Add tomato sauce, sun-dried tomatoes, wine and lemon peel. Cover and cook on LOW setting for 4 hours (or on HIGH for 2 hours).

2. Add mushrooms and *1 cup* French Fried Onions. Cover and cook on LOW setting for 2 hours (or on HIGH for 1 hour) until chicken is no longer pink near bone. Remove chicken to heated platter. Skim fat from sauce.

3. Serve chicken with hot cooked rice or pasta, if desired. Spoon sauce on top and sprinkle with remaining onions.

Makes 4 servings

Chicken Enchilada Roll-Ups

Prep Time: 20 minutes   **Cook Time:** 7¼ to 8¼ hours

1½ pounds boneless skinless
    chicken breasts

½ cup plus 2 tablespoons all-
    purpose flour, divided

½ teaspoon salt

2 tablespoons butter

1 cup chicken broth

1 small onion, diced

¼ to ½ cup canned jalapeño
    peppers, sliced

½ teaspoon dried oregano

2 tablespoons whipping cream
    or milk

6 flour tortillas (7 to 8 inches)

6 thin slices American cheese or
    American cheese with
    jalapeño peppers

1. Cut each chicken breast lengthwise into 2 or 3 strips. Combine ½ cup flour and salt in resealable plastic food storage bag. Add chicken strips and shake to coat with flour mixture. Melt butter in large skillet over medium heat. Brown chicken strips in batches 2 to 3 minutes per side. Place chicken into slow cooker.

2. Add chicken broth to skillet and scrape up any browned bits. Pour broth mixture into slow cooker. Add onion, jalapeño peppers and oregano. Cover; cook on LOW 7 to 8 hours or on HIGH 3 to 4 hours.

3. Blend remaining 2 tablespoons flour and cream in small bowl until smooth. Stir into chicken mixture. Cook, uncovered, on HIGH 15 minutes or until thickened. Spoon chicken mixture onto center of flour tortillas. Top with 1 cheese slice. Fold up tortillas and serve.   *Makes 6 servings*

Serving Suggestion: This rich creamy chicken mixture can also be served over hot cooked rice.

Thai-Style Chicken Thighs

Cook Time: 6¼ to 7¼ hours

1 teaspoon ground ginger

½ teaspoon salt

¼ teaspoon ground red pepper

6 bone-in chicken thighs (about 2¼ pounds), skinned

1 medium onion, chopped

3 cloves garlic, minced

⅓ cup canned coconut milk

¼ cup creamy peanut butter

2 tablespoons soy sauce

1 tablespoon cornstarch

2 tablespoons water

3 cups hot cooked couscous or yellow rice

¼ cup chopped cilantro

Lime wedges (optional)

1. Coat slow cooker with cooking spray. Combine ginger, salt and red pepper; sprinkle over meaty sides of chicken. Place onion and garlic in slow cooker; top with chicken. Whisk together coconut milk, peanut butter and soy sauce; pour over chicken. Cover and cook on LOW 6 to 7 hours or on HIGH 3 to 4 hours or until chicken is tender.

2. With slotted spoon, transfer chicken to serving bowl; cover with foil to keep warm. Turn slow cooker to HIGH. Combine cornstarch with water until smooth. Stir into juices; cover and cook 15 minutes or until sauce is slightly thickened. Spoon sauce over chicken. Serve chicken over couscous; top with cilantro. Serve with lime wedges, if desired.

Makes 6 servings

South-of-the-Border Cumin Chicken

Cook Time: 8 hours

1 package (16 ounces) frozen bell pepper stir-fry mixture, thawed *or* 3 bell peppers, thinly sliced*

4 chicken drumsticks, skin removed

4 chicken thighs, skin removed

1 can (14½ ounces) stewed tomatoes

1 tablespoon green pepper sauce

2 teaspoons sugar

1¾ teaspoons ground cumin, divided

1¼ teaspoons salt

1 teaspoon dried oregano

¼ cup chopped fresh cilantro

1 to 2 medium limes, cut into wedges

If using fresh bell peppers, add 1 small onion, chopped.

1. Place bell pepper mixture in slow cooker; arrange chicken on top of pepper mixture.

2. Combine tomatoes, pepper sauce, sugar, 1 teaspoon cumin, salt and oregano in large bowl. Pour over chicken mixture. Cover; cook on LOW 8 hours or on HIGH 4 hours or until chicken is tender.

3. Place chicken in shallow serving bowl. Stir remaining ¾ teaspoon cumin into tomato mixture and pour over chicken. Sprinkle with cilantro and serve with lime wedges. Serve over cooked rice or with toasted corn tortillas, if desired.

Makes 4 servings

Chutney Curried Chicken with Yogurt Sauce

Cook Time: 5¼ to 6¼ hours

1 container (6 to 8 ounces) plain low-fat yogurt

2 teaspoons curry powder

1 teaspoon garlic salt

⅛ teaspoon ground red pepper

4 large bone-in chicken breasts, skinned (2 to 2¼ pounds)

1 small onion, sliced

⅓ cup mango chutney (chop large pieces of mango, if necessary)

1 tablespoon lime juice

2 cloves garlic, minced

2 tablespoons cornstarch

2 tablespoons water

3 cups hot cooked lo mein noodles or linguini

Chopped cilantro, chopped peanuts or toasted coconut (optional)

1. Place yogurt in paper-towel-lined strainer over a bowl. Drain in refrigerator until serving time.

2. Sprinkle curry powder, garlic salt and red pepper over chicken breasts. Place onion in slow cooker; top with chicken. Combine chutney, lime juice and garlic; spoon over chicken. Cover and cook on LOW 5 to 6 hours or on HIGH 2½ to 3 hours or until chicken is tender.

3. With slotted spoon, transfer chicken to serving platter; cover with foil to keep warm. Turn slow cooker to HIGH. Combine cornstarch with water until smooth. Stir into juices; cover and cook 15 minutes or until thickened. Spoon sauce over chicken; serve over noodles. Top with thickened yogurt and garnish with cilantro, peanuts or coconut, if desired.

Makes 4 servings

Slow-Simmered Curried Chicken

Prep Time: 15 to 20 minutes   **Cook Time:** 5¼ to 6¼ hours

1½ cups chopped onions

1 medium green bell pepper, chopped

1 pound boneless skinless chicken breasts or thighs, cut into bite-size pieces

1 cup medium salsa

2 teaspoons grated fresh ginger

½ teaspoon garlic powder

½ teaspoon red pepper flakes

¼ cup chopped fresh cilantro

1 teaspoon sugar

1 teaspoon curry powder

¾ teaspoon salt

Hot cooked rice

1. Place onions and bell pepper in slow cooker. Top with chicken. Combine salsa, ginger, garlic powder and pepper flakes in small bowl; spoon over chicken.

2. Cover; cook on LOW 5 to 6 hours or until chicken is tender.

3. Combine cilantro, sugar, curry powder and salt in small bowl; stir into slow cooker. Cover; cook on HIGH 15 minutes or until hot. Serve over rice.   *Makes 4 servings*

Coconut Chicken Curry

Cook Time: 6½ to 8½ hours

1 tablespoon vegetable oil

4 boneless skinless chicken breasts

3 medium potatoes, peeled and chopped

1 medium onion, sliced

1 can (14 ounces) coconut milk

1 cup chicken broth

1½ teaspoons curry powder

1 teaspoon hot pepper sauce

½ teaspoon salt

¼ to ½ teaspoon black pepper

1 package (10 ounces) frozen peas, thawed

1. Heat oil in large skillet over medium-high heat. Brown chicken breasts on both sides. Place potatoes and onion in slow cooker. Top with chicken breasts.

2. Combine coconut milk, broth, curry powder, pepper sauce, salt and pepper in medium bowl. Pour over chicken. Cover; cook on LOW 6 to 8 hours.

3. Add peas to slow cooker. Cook, covered, 30 minutes or until chicken is tender. Serve over hot cooked rice, if desired.

Makes 4 servings

Chicken with Italian Sausage

Prep Time: 15 minutes   **Cook Time:** 5 to 6 hours

10 ounces bulk mild or hot Italian sausage

6 boneless skinless chicken thighs

1 can (about 15 ounces) white beans, rinsed and drained

1 can (about 15 ounces) red beans, rinsed and drained

1 cup chicken broth

1 medium onion, chopped

½ teaspoon salt

½ teaspoon black pepper

Chopped fresh parsley

1. Brown sausage in large skillet over medium-high heat, stirring to separate; drain fat. Spoon into slow cooker.

2. Trim fat from chicken. Place chicken, beans, broth, onion, salt and pepper in slow cooker. Cover; cook on LOW 5 to 6 hours.

3. Adjust seasonings, if desired. Slice each chicken thigh on the diagonal. Serve with sausage and beans. Garnish with parsley, if desired.

Makes 6 servings

Tender Asian-Style Chicken

Prep Time: 15 minutes   **Cook Time:** 5 to 6 hours

¼ cup all-purpose flour

½ teaspoon black pepper

6 to 8 boneless skinless chicken thighs

1 tablespoon vegetable oil

¼ cup soy sauce

2 tablespoons rice wine vinegar

2 tablespoons ketchup

1 tablespoon brown sugar

1 clove garlic, minced

½ teaspoon grated fresh ginger *or* ¼ teaspoon ground ginger

¼ teaspoon red pepper flakes

Hot cooked rice

Chopped fresh cilantro (optional)

1. Combine flour and black pepper in resealable plastic food storage bag. Add chicken; shake to coat with flour mixture.

2. Heat oil in large skillet over medium-high heat. Brown chicken about 2 minutes on each side. Place chicken in slow cooker. Combine soy sauce, vinegar, ketchup, sugar, garlic, ginger and pepper flakes in small bowl; pour over chicken. Cook on LOW 5 to 6 hours. Serve with rice and garnish with cilantro, if desired.

Makes 4 to 6 servings

Turkey with Pecan-Cherry Stuffing

Prep Time: 20 minutes   **Cook Time:** 5 to 6 hours

1 fresh or frozen boneless turkey breast (about 3 to 4 pounds)

2 cups cooked rice

⅓ cup chopped pecans

⅓ cup dried cherries or cranberries

1 teaspoon poultry seasoning

¼ cup peach, apricot or plum preserves

1 teaspoon Worcestershire sauce

1. Thaw turkey breast, if frozen. Remove and discard skin. Cut slices three fourths of the way through turkey at 1-inch intervals.

2. Stir together rice, pecans, cherries and poultry seasoning in large bowl. Stuff rice mixture between slices. If needed, skewer turkey lengthwise to hold together.

3. Place turkey in slow cooker. Cover; cook on LOW 5 to 6 hours or until turkey registers 170°F on meat thermometer inserted into thickest part of breast, not touching stuffing.

4. Stir together preserves and Worcestershire sauce. Spoon over turkey. Cover; let stand for 5 minutes. Remove and discard skewer, if used.

Makes 8 servings

Serving Suggestion: Serve with asparagus spears, crescent rolls and spinach salad.

Mexicali Chicken

Prep Time: 10 minutes   **Cook Time:** 7¼ to 8¼ hours

2 medium green bell peppers, cut into thin strips

1 large onion, quartered and thinly sliced

4 chicken thighs, skin removed

4 chicken drumsticks, skin removed

1 tablespoon chili powder

2 teaspoons dried oregano

1 jar (16 ounces) chipotle salsa

½ cup ketchup

2 teaspoons ground cumin

½ teaspoon salt

Hot cooked noodles

1. Place bell peppers and onion in slow cooker; top with chicken. Sprinkle chili powder and oregano evenly over chicken. Add salsa. Cover; cook on LOW 7 to 8 hours or on HIGH 3 to 4 hours.

2. Remove chicken pieces to serving bowl; keep warm. Stir ketchup, cumin and salt into liquid in slow cooker. Cook, uncovered, on HIGH 15 minutes or until hot.

3. Pour mixture over chicken. Serve with noodles.   *Makes 4 servings*

Tip: For thicker sauce, blend 1 tablespoon cornstarch and 2 tablespoons water until smooth. Stir into cooking liquid with ketchup, cumin and salt.

Appetizers & Snacks

Parmesan Ranch Snack Mix

Prep Time: 5 minutes   **Cook Time:** 3½ hours

3 cups corn or rice cereal squares

2 cups oyster crackers

1 package (5 ounces) bagel chips, broken in half

1½ cups mini-pretzel twists

1 cup pistachio nuts

2 tablespoons grated Parmesan cheese

¼ cup (½ stick) butter, melted

1 package (1 ounce) dry ranch salad dressing mix

½ teaspoon garlic powder

1. Combine cereal, oyster crackers, bagel chips, pretzels, pistachio nuts and Parmesan cheese in slow cooker; mix gently.

2. Combine butter, salad dressing mix and garlic powder in small bowl. Pour over cereal mixture; toss lightly to coat. Cover; cook on LOW 3 hours.

3. Remove cover; stir gently. Cook, uncovered, 30 minutes.

Makes about 9 cups snack mix

Chili con Queso

1 pound pasteurized process cheese spread, cut into cubes

1 can (10 ounces) diced tomatoes with green chilies, undrained

1 cup sliced green onions

2 teaspoons ground coriander

2 teaspoons ground cumin

¾ teaspoon hot pepper sauce

Green onion strips (optional)

Hot pepper slices (optional)

Tortilla chips

1. Combine cheese spread, tomatoes with juice, green onions, coriander and cumin in 1½-quart slow cooker; stir until well blended.

2. Cover; cook on LOW 2 to 3 hours or until hot.* Stir in pepper sauce.

3. Garnish with green onion strips and hot pepper slices, if desired. Serve with tortilla chips.

Makes 3 cups

*Dip will be very hot; use caution when serving.

Serving Suggestion: Serve Chili con Queso with tortilla chips. Or, for something different, cut pita bread into triangles and toast in preheated 400°F oven for 5 minutes or until crisp.

Creamy Artichoke-Parmesan Dip

Cook Time: 2 hours

2 cans (14 ounces each)
    artichoke hearts, drained
    and chopped
2 cups (8 ounces) shredded
    mozzarella cheese
1½ cups grated Parmesan cheese
1½ cups mayonnaise
½ cup finely chopped onion
½ teaspoon dried oregano
¼ teaspoon garlic powder
4 pita breads
    Assorted cut-up vegetables

1. Combine artichokes, cheeses, mayonnaise, onion, oregano and garlic powder in 1½-quart slow cooker; mix well.

2. Cover; cook on LOW 2 hours.

3. Meanwhile, cut pita breads into wedges. Arrange pita breads and vegetables on platter; serve with warm dip.

Makes 4 cups dip

Cranberry-Barbecue Chicken Wings

Prep Time: 20 minutes   **Cook Time:** 4 to 5 hours

3 pounds chicken wings
    Salt and pepper
1 container (12 ounces)
    cranberry-orange relish
½ cup barbecue sauce
2 tablespoons quick-cooking
    tapioca
1 tablespoon prepared mustard
    Hot cooked rice (optional)

1. Preheat broiler. Cut off chicken wing tips; discard. Cut each wing in half at joint. Place chicken on rack in broiler pan; season with salt and pepper. Broil 4 to 5 inches from heat for 10 to 12 minutes or until browned, turning once. Transfer chicken to slow cooker.

2. Stir together relish, barbecue sauce, tapioca and mustard in small bowl. Pour over chicken. Cover; cook on LOW 4 to 5 hours. Serve with hot cooked rice, if desired.

Makes about 16 appetizer servings

Spicy Sweet & Sour Cocktail Franks

Prep Time: 8 minutes   **Cook Time:** 2 to 3 hours

2 packages (8 ounces each) cocktail franks

½ cup ketchup or chili sauce

½ cup apricot preserves

1 teaspoon hot pepper sauce

1. Combine all ingredients in 1½-quart slow cooker; mix well. Cover; cook on LOW 2 to 3 hours.

2. Serve warm or at room temperature with cocktail picks and additional hot pepper sauce, if desired.   *Makes about 4 dozen franks*

Maple-Glazed Meatballs

Prep Time: 10 minutes   **Cook Time:** 5 to 6 hours

1½ cups ketchup

1 cup maple syrup or maple-flavored syrup

⅓ cup reduced-sodium soy sauce

1 tablespoon quick-cooking tapioca

1½ teaspoons ground allspice

1 teaspoon dry mustard

2 packages (about 16 ounces each) frozen fully-cooked meatballs, partially thawed

1 can (20 ounces) pineapple chunks in juice, drained

1. Combine ketchup, maple syrup, soy sauce, tapioca, allspice and mustard in slow cooker.

2. Separate meatballs. Carefully stir meatballs and pineapple chunks into ketchup mixture.

3. Cover; cook on LOW 5 to 6 hours. Stir before serving. Serve with cocktail picks.

Makes about 48 meatballs

Variation: Serve over hot cooked rice for an entrée.

Honey-Mustard Chicken Wings

Prep Time: 20 minutes   **Cook Time:** 4 to 5 hours

3 pounds chicken wings

1 teaspoon salt

1 teaspoon black pepper

½ cup honey

½ cup barbecue sauce

2 tablespoons spicy brown mustard

1 clove garlic, minced

3 to 4 thin lemon slices

1. Cut off chicken wing tips; discard. Cut each wing at joint to make two pieces. Sprinkle salt and pepper on both sides of chicken. Place wing pieces on broiler rack. Broil 4 to 5 inches from heat about 10 minutes, turning halfway through cooking time. Place broiled chicken wings in slow cooker.

2. Combine honey, barbecue sauce, mustard and garlic in small bowl; mix well. Pour sauce over chicken wings. Top with lemon slices. Cover; cook on LOW 4 to 5 hours.

3. Remove and discard lemon slices. Serve wings with sauce.   *Makes about 24 appetizers*

Caponata

Cook Time: 7 to 8 hours

1 medium eggplant (about
    1 pound), peeled and cut
    into ½-inch pieces

1 can (14½ ounces) diced
    Italian plum tomatoes,
    undrained

1 medium onion, chopped

1 red bell pepper, cut into
    ½-inch pieces

½ cup medium-hot salsa

¼ cup olive oil

2 tablespoons capers, drained

2 tablespoons balsamic vinegar

3 cloves garlic, minced

1 teaspoon dried oregano

¼ teaspoon salt

⅓ cup packed fresh basil, cut
    into thin strips

   Toasted sliced Italian or
    French bread

1. Mix eggplant, tomatoes with juice, onion, bell pepper, salsa, oil, capers, vinegar, garlic, oregano and salt in slow cooker.

2. Cover; cook on LOW 7 to 8 hours or until vegetables are tender.

3. Stir in basil. Serve at room temperature with toasted bread. *Makes about 5 cups*

Honey-Sauced Chicken Wings

Cook Time: 4 to 5 hours

3 pounds chicken wings

1 teaspoon salt

½ teaspoon black pepper

1 cup honey

½ cup soy sauce

¼ cup chopped onion

¼ cup ketchup

2 tablespoons vegetable oil

2 cloves garlic, minced

¼ teaspoon red pepper flakes

Toasted sesame seeds
  (optional)

1. Preheat broiler. Cut off and discard chicken wing tips. Cut each wing at joint to make two sections. Sprinkle wing parts with salt and pepper. Place wings on broiler pan. Broil 4 to 5 inches from heat 10 minutes per side or until chicken is brown. Place chicken into slow cooker.

2. For sauce, combine honey, soy sauce, onion, ketchup, oil, garlic and pepper flakes in bowl. Pour over chicken wings.

3. Cover; cook on LOW 4 to 5 hours or on HIGH 2 to 2½ hours. Garnish with sesame seeds, if desired. *Makes about 32 appetizers*

Festive Bacon & Cheese Dip

Cook Time: 1 hour

2 packages (8 ounces each) cream cheese, cut into cubes

4 cups (16 ounces) shredded Colby-Jack cheese

1 cup half-and-half

2 tablespoons prepared mustard

1 tablespoon chopped onion

2 teaspoons Worcestershire sauce

½ teaspoon salt

¼ teaspoon hot pepper sauce

1 pound bacon, crisp-cooked and crumbled

1. Combine cream cheese, Colby-Jack cheese, half-and-half, mustard, onion, Worcestershire sauce, salt and hot pepper sauce in 1½-quart slow cooker.

2. Cover; cook, stirring occasionally, on LOW 1 hour or until cheese melts.

3. Stir in bacon; adjust seasonings. Serve with crusty bread or vegetable dippers.

Makes about 4 cups dip

The Best of the Rest

Gingered Pineapple & Cranberries

Cook Time: 3¼ hours (HIGH)

2 cans (20 ounces each) pineapple chunks in juice, undrained

1 cup dried sweetened cranberries

½ cup packed brown sugar

1 teaspoon curry powder, divided

1 teaspoon grated fresh ginger, divided

¼ teaspoon red pepper flakes

2 tablespoons water

1 tablespoon cornstarch

1. Place pineapple with juice, cranberries, brown sugar, ½ teaspoon curry powder, ½ teaspoon ginger and pepper flakes into 1½-quart slow cooker.

2. Cover; cook on HIGH 3 hours.

3. Combine water, cornstarch, remaining ½ teaspoon curry powder and ½ teaspoon ginger in small bowl; stir until cornstarch is dissolved. Add to pineapple mixture. Cook, uncovered, on HIGH 15 minutes or until thickened. *Makes 4½ cups*

Variation: Substitute 2 cans (20 ounces each) pineapple tidbits in heavy syrup for pineapple and brown sugar.

Honey Whole-Grain Bread

Cook Time: 3 hours (HIGH)

3 cups whole wheat bread flour, divided

2 cups warm (not hot) milk

¾ to 1 cup all-purpose flour, divided

¼ cup honey

2 tablespoons vegetable oil

1 package active dry yeast

¾ teaspoon salt

1. Spray 1-quart casserole, soufflé dish or other high-sided baking pan that will fit in your slow cooker with nonstick cooking spray. Combine 1½ cups whole wheat flour, milk, ½ cup all-purpose flour, honey, oil, yeast and salt in large bowl. Beat with electric mixer at medium speed 2 minutes.

2. Add remaining 1½ cups whole wheat flour and ¼ cup to ½ cup all-purpose flour until dough is no longer sticky. (If mixer has difficulty mixing dough, mix in remaining flours with wooden spoon.) Transfer to prepared dish.

3. Make foil handles (see page 190). Place dish in slow cooker. Cover; cook on HIGH 3 hours or until edges are browned.

4. Use foil handles to lift dish from slow cooker. Let stand 5 minutes. Remove from dish to wire rack to cool.

Makes 8 to 10 servings

Mulled Apple Cider

Cook Time: 2½ to 3 hours (HIGH)

2 quarts bottled apple cider or juice (not unfiltered)

¼ cup packed light brown sugar

1 square (8 inches) double-thickness cheesecloth

8 allspice berries

4 cinnamon sticks, broken into halves

12 whole cloves

1 large orange

Additional cinnamon sticks (optional)

1. Combine apple cider and brown sugar in 2½ to 3-quart slow cooker. Rinse cheesecloth; squeeze out water. Wrap allspice berries and cinnamon stick halves in cheesecloth; tie securely with cotton string or strip of cheesecloth. Stick cloves randomly into orange; cut orange into quarters. Place spice bag and orange quarters in cider mixture.

2. Cover; cook on HIGH 2½ to 3 hours.

3. Once cooked, cider may be turned to LOW and kept warm up to 3 additional hours. Remove and discard spice bag and orange before serving. Ladle cider into mugs. Garnish with additional cinnamon sticks, if desired.

Makes 10 servings

Tip: To make inserting cloves into the orange a little easier, first pierce the orange skin with the point of wooden skewer. Remove the skewer and insert a clove.

Chunky Sweet Spiced Apple Butter

Cook Time: 8 hours

4 cups (about 1¼ pounds) peeled, chopped Granny Smith apples

¾ cup packed dark brown sugar

2 tablespoons balsamic vinegar

4 tablespoons butter, divided

1 tablespoon ground cinnamon

½ teaspoon salt

¼ teaspoon ground cloves

1½ teaspoons vanilla

1. Combine apples, sugar, vinegar, 2 tablespoons butter, cinnamon, salt and cloves in 1½-quart slow cooker. Cover; cook on LOW 8 hours.

2. Stir in remaining 2 tablespoons butter and vanilla. Cool completely. *Makes 2 cups*

Serving Suggestions: Serve with roasted meats or spread on toast.

Skinny Cornbread

Cook Time: 3 to 4 hours

1¼ cups all-purpose flour

¾ cup yellow cornmeal

¼ cup sugar

1 teaspoon baking powder

1 teaspoon baking soda

1 teaspoon seasoned salt

1 cup buttermilk

¼ cup cholesterol-free egg substitute

¼ cup canola oil

1. Preheat slow cooker on HIGH. Grease 2-quart soufflé dish

2. Sift together flour, cornmeal, sugar, baking powder, baking soda and seasoned salt in large bowl. Make well in center of dry mixture. Pour in buttermilk, egg substitute and oil. Mix just until dry ingredients are moistened. Pour batter into prepared dish.

3. Cover with foil or lid. Place on rack or metal trivet in preheated slow cooker. Cover; cook on LOW 3 to 4 hours or on HIGH 30 minutes to 2 hours or until edges are golden and knife inserted into center comes out clean. *Makes 8 servings*

Note: You may wish to cook the cornbread with slow cooker lid slightly ajar to allow any condensation to evaporate.

Peasant Potatoes

Cook Time: 6 to 8 hours

¼ cup (½ stick) butter

1 large sweet onion, chopped

2 large cloves garlic, chopped

½ pound beef smoked sausage, cut into ¾-inch slices

1 teaspoon dried oregano

6 medium potatoes, preferably Yukon Gold, cut into 1½- to 2-inch pieces

Salt and black pepper

2 cups sliced savoy or other green cabbage

1 cup diced or sliced roasted red pepper

½ cup shaved fresh Parmesan cheese

1. Melt butter in large skillet over medium heat. Add onion and garlic; cook and stir 5 minutes or until onion is transparent. Stir in sausage and oregano. Cook 5 minutes. Stir in potatoes, salt and black pepper; mix well. Transfer mixture to slow cooker.

2. Cover; cook on LOW 6 to 8 hours or on HIGH 3 to 4 hours, stirring every hour. Add cabbage and roasted red peppers during last 30 minutes of cooking.

3. Top with Parmesan cheese before serving.

Makes 6 side-dish servings

Warm & Spicy Fruit Punch

Prep Time: 10 minutes   **Cook Time:** 5 to 6 hours

4 cinnamon sticks

1 orange

1 teaspoon whole allspice

½ teaspoon whole cloves

7 cups water

1 can (12 ounces) frozen cranberry-raspberry juice concentrate, thawed

1 can (6 ounces) frozen lemonade concentrate, thawed

2 cans (5½ ounces each) apricot nectar

1. Break cinnamon sticks into pieces. Using vegetable peeler, remove strips of orange peel. Squeeze juice from orange; set aside.

2. Tie cinnamon sticks, orange peel, allspice and cloves in cheesecloth bag.

3. Combine orange juice, water, juice concentrates and apricot nectar in 4-quart slow cooker; add spice bag. Cover; cook on LOW 5 to 6 hours.

4. Remove and discard spice bag.

Makes about 14 servings

Cran-Orange Acorn Squash

Cook Time: 2½ hours

3 small acorn or carnival squash

5 tablespoons instant brown rice

3 tablespoons minced onion

3 tablespoons diced celery

3 tablespoons dried cranberries

Pinch ground or dried sage

1 teaspoon butter, cut into bits

3 tablespoons orange juice

½ cup water

1. Slice off tops of squash and enough of bottoms so squash will sit upright. Scoop out seeds and discard; set squash aside.

2. Combine rice, onion, celery, cranberries and sage in small bowl. Stuff each squash with rice mixture; dot with butter. Pour 1 tablespoon orange juice into each squash over stuffing. Stand squash in slow cooker. Pour water into bottom of slow cooker.

3. Cover; cook on LOW 2½ hours or until squash are tender.

Makes 6 servings

Tip: The skin of squash can defy even the sharpest knives. To make slicing easier, microwave the whole squash at HIGH 5 minutes to soften the skin.

Mocha Supreme

2 quarts strong brewed coffee

½ cup instant hot chocolate beverage mix

1 cinnamon stick, broken into halves

1 cup whipping cream

1 tablespoon powdered sugar

1. Place coffee, hot chocolate mix and cinnamon stick halves in 3- to 3½-quart slow cooker; stir. Cover; cook on HIGH 2 to 2½ hours or until hot. Remove and discard cinnamon stick halves.

2. Beat cream in medium bowl with electric mixer on high speed until soft peaks form. Add powdered sugar; beat until stiff peaks form. Ladle hot beverage into mugs; top with whipped cream.

Makes 8 servings

Note: You can whip cream faster if you first chill the beaters and bowls in the freezer for 15 minutes.

Mulled Cranberry Tea

Prep Time: 10 minutes   **Cook Time:** 2 to 3 hours

2 tea bags

1 cup boiling water

1 bottle (48 ounces) cranberry juice

½ cup dried cranberries (optional)

⅓ cup sugar

1 large lemon, cut into ¼-inch slices

4 cinnamon sticks

6 whole cloves

Additional thin lemon slices and cinnamon sticks for garnish

1. Place tea bags in slow cooker. Pour boiling water over tea bags; cover and let stand 5 minutes. Remove and discard tea bags. Stir in cranberry juice, cranberries, if desired, sugar, lemon slices, 4 cinnamon sticks and cloves. Cover; cook on LOW 2 to 3 hours or on HIGH 1 to 2 hours.

2. Remove and discard lemon slices, cinnamon sticks and cloves. Serve in warm mug with additional fresh lemon slice and cinnamon stick.

Makes 8 servings

Spiced Apple & Cranberry Compote

Cook Time: 4 to 5 hours

2½ cups cranberry juice cocktail

1 package (6 ounces) dried apples

½ cup (2 ounces) dried cranberries

½ cup Rhine wine or apple juice

½ cup honey

2 cinnamon sticks, broken into halves

Frozen yogurt or ice cream (optional)

Additional cinnamon sticks (optional)

Mix juice, apples, cranberries, wine, honey and cinnamon stick halves in slow cooker. Cover and cook on LOW 4 to 5 hours or until liquid is absorbed and fruit is tender. Remove and discard cinnamon stick halves. Ladle compote into bowls. Serve warm, at room temperature or chilled with frozen yogurt or ice cream, if desired. Garnish with additional cinnamon sticks, if desired.

Makes 6 servings

Potato Casserole with Creamy Cheese Sauce

Cook Time: 3 hours (HIGH)

2 pounds russet potatoes, sliced

2 medium yellow squash, cut into ¼-inch slices

1 cup chopped onions

1 cup chopped red bell pepper

⅓ cup water

2 tablespoons butter

¾ teaspoon dried thyme

¾ teaspoon salt

¼ teaspoon black pepper

⅛ teaspoon ground red pepper

½ cup half-and-half

8 slices processed American cheese

1. Place all ingredients into slow cooker except half-and-half and cheese in the order listed. Cover; cook on HIGH 3 hours.

2. Remove vegetables with slotted spoon and place in serving bowl. Stir half-and-half and cheese into slow cooker. Cover; cook 5 minutes or until cheese melts. Whisk until well blended; pour over vegetables.

Makes 8 to 10 servings

Whole-Grain Banana Bread

Cook Time: 2 to 3 hours (HIGH)

¼ cup plus 2 tablespoons wheat germ, divided

⅔ cup butter, softened

1 cup sugar

2 eggs

1 cup mashed bananas (2 to 3 bananas)

1 teaspoon vanilla

1 cup all-purpose flour

1 cup whole wheat pastry flour

1 teaspoon baking soda

½ teaspoon salt

½ cup chopped walnuts or pecans (optional)

1. Spray 1-quart casserole, soufflé dish or other high-sided baking pan with nonstick cooking spray. Sprinkle dish with about 2 tablespoons wheat germ.

2. Beat butter and sugar in large bowl on medium speed of electric mixer until fluffy. Gradually beat in eggs. Add bananas and vanilla; beat until smooth.

3. Gradually stir in flours, remaining ¼ cup wheat germ, baking soda and salt. Stir in nuts, if desired. Pour batter into prepared dish; place in slow cooker. Cover; cook on HIGH 2 to 3 hours or until edges begin to brown and toothpick inserted into center comes out clean.

4. Remove dish from slow cooker. Cool on wire rack about 10 minutes. Remove bread from dish and cool completely on wire rack.

Makes 8 to 10 servings

EASY SLOW-COOKER

RECIPES

Contents

Simple Soups

Easy Corn Chowder

Prep Time: 15 minutes   **Cook Time:** 7 to 8 hours

2 cans (14½ ounces each) chicken broth

1 bag (16 ounces) frozen corn kernels, thawed

3 small potatoes, peeled and cut into ½-inch pieces

1 red bell pepper, diced

1 medium onion, diced

1 rib celery, sliced

½ teaspoon salt

½ teaspoon black pepper

¼ teaspoon ground coriander

½ cup whipping cream

8 slices bacon, crisp-cooked and crumbled

1. Place broth, corn, potatoes, bell pepper, onion, celery, salt, black pepper and coriander into slow cooker. Cover; cook on LOW 7 to 8 hours.

2. Partially mash soup mixture with potato masher to thicken. Stir in cream; cook on HIGH, uncovered, until hot. Adjust seasonings, if desired. Garnish with bacon.

Makes 6 servings

Vegetable & Red Lentil Soup

Cook Time: 8 hours

1 can (14½ ounces) vegetable broth

1 can (14½ ounces) diced tomatoes, undrained

2 medium zucchini or yellow summer squash (or 1 of each), diced

1 red or yellow bell pepper, diced

½ cup thinly sliced carrots

½ cup red lentils, rinsed*

½ teaspoon salt

½ teaspoon sugar

¼ teaspoon black pepper

2 tablespoons chopped fresh basil or thyme

½ cup croutons or shredded cheese (optional)

If you have difficulty finding red lentils, substitute brown lentils instead.

1. Coat slow cooker with cooking spray. Combine broth, tomatoes with juice, zucchini, bell pepper, carrots, lentils, salt, sugar and black pepper in slow cooker; mix well.

2. Cover and cook on LOW 8 hours or on HIGH 4 hours or until lentils and vegetables are tender. Before serving, top with basil and croutons, if desired. *Makes 4 servings*

Chicken and Vegetable Chowder

Cook Time: 5¼ to 6¼ hours

1 pound boneless skinless
chicken breasts, cut into
1-inch pieces

1 can (14½ ounces) reduced-
sodium chicken broth

1 can (10¾ ounces) condensed
cream of potato soup,
undiluted

1 package (10 ounces) frozen
broccoli cuts, thawed

1 cup sliced carrots

1 jar (4½ ounces) sliced
mushrooms, drained

½ cup chopped onion

½ cup frozen corn

2 cloves garlic, minced

½ teaspoon dried thyme

⅓ cup half-and-half

1. Combine chicken, broth, soup, broccoli, carrots, mushrooms, onion, corn, garlic and thyme in slow cooker; mix well.

2. Cover; cook on LOW 5 to 6 hours.

3. Stir in half-and-half. Cover; cook on HIGH 15 minutes or until heated through.

Makes 6 servings

Variation: Add ½ cup (2 ounces) shredded Swiss or Cheddar cheese just before serving, stirring over LOW heat until melted.

Slow Cooker Cheese Soup

Cook Time: 2½ to 3½ hours

2 cans (10¾ ounces each) condensed cream of celery soup, undiluted

4 cups (16 ounces) shredded Cheddar cheese

1 teaspoon paprika

1 teaspoon Worcestershire sauce

1¼ cups half-and-half

Salt and black pepper

1. Combine soup, cheese, paprika and Worcestershire sauce in slow cooker.

2. Cover; cook on LOW 2 to 3 hours.

3. Add half-and-half; stir until blended. Cover; cook another 20 minutes. Season to taste with salt and pepper. Garnish as desired. *Makes 4 servings*

Tortilla Soup

Prep Time: 10 minutes   **Cook Time:** 6¼ to 8¼ hours

2 cans (14½ ounces each) chicken broth

1 can (14½ ounces) diced tomatoes with jalapeño peppers, undrained

2 cups chopped carrots

2 cups frozen whole kernel corn, thawed

1½ cups chopped onions

1 can (8 ounces) tomato sauce

1 tablespoon chili powder

1 teaspoon ground cumin

¼ teaspoon garlic powder

2 cups chopped cooked chicken (optional)

Shredded Monterey Jack cheese

Tortilla chips, broken

1. Combine broth, tomatoes with juice, carrots, corn, onions, tomato sauce, chili powder, cumin and garlic powder in 4-quart slow cooker. Cover; cook on LOW 6 to 8 hours.

2. Stir in chicken, if desired. Cook until heated through. Ladle into bowls. Top each serving with cheese and tortilla chips.

Makes 6 servings

No-Chop Black Bean Soup

Cook Time: 8 to 10 hours

3 cans (15 ounces each) black beans, rinsed and drained

1 package (12 ounces) frozen diced green bell peppers, thawed

2 cups frozen chopped onions, thawed

2 cans (14½ ounces each) chicken broth

1 can (14½ ounces) diced tomatoes with pepper, celery and onion, undrained

1 teaspoon bottled minced garlic

1½ teaspoons ground cumin, divided

2 tablespoons olive oil

¾ teaspoon salt

1. Combine beans, bell peppers, onions, broth, tomatoes with juice, garlic and 1 teaspoon cumin in 4- to 5-quart slow cooker.

2. Cover; cook on LOW 8 to 10 hours or on HIGH 5 hours.

3. Stir in oil, salt and remaining ½ teaspoon cumin just before serving. *Makes 8 servings*

Simple Turkey Soup

Cook Time: 3 to 4 hours (HIGH)

2 pounds ground turkey, cooked and drained

1 can (28 ounces) tomatoes, undrained

2 cans (14½ ounces each) beef broth

1 bag (16 ounces) frozen mixed soup vegetables (such as carrots, beans, okra, corn or onion), thawed

½ cup uncooked barley

1 teaspoon salt

1 teaspoon dried thyme

½ teaspoon ground coriander

Black pepper

1. Combine turkey, tomatoes with juice, broth, vegetables, barley, salt, thyme, coriander and pepper in 5-quart slow cooker. Add water to cover.

2. Cover; cook on HIGH 3 to 4 hours or until barley and vegetables are tender.

Makes 8 servings

Southwestern Chicken Chowder

Cook Time: 1 to 2 hours

1 can (15 ounces) VEG•ALL® Original Mixed Vegetables, drained

2 cups cubed cooked chicken

1 medium sweet red pepper, seeded & chopped

1½ cups whole milk

1 can (10¾ ounces) cream of chicken soup

1 cup mild green salsa, or thick and chunky salsa

1 tablespoon fresh lime juice

1 can (15½ ounces) mild chili beans

1 tablespoon chopped fresh cilantro (optional)

Combine all ingredients except cilantro in a 2- to 3-quart slow cooker. Cook, covered, on LOW for 1 to 2 hours or until heated through.

Add cilantro and serve. *Makes 6 to 8 servings*

Sandwiches & Wraps

Slow-Cooked Kielbasa in a Bun

Prep Time: 10 minutes   **Cook Time:** 7 to 8 hours

4 kielbasa sausages
1 large onion, thinly sliced
1 large green bell pepper, cut
    into strips
¼ teaspoon salt
¼ teaspoon dried thyme
¼ teaspoon black pepper
½ cup chicken broth
4 hoagie rolls, split

1. Brown kielbasa in nonstick skillet over medium-high heat 3 to 4 minutes. Place kielbasa in slow cooker. Add onion, bell pepper, salt, thyme and black pepper. Stir in chicken broth.

2. Cover; cook on LOW 7 to 8 hours.

3. Place kielbasa into rolls. Top with onion and bell pepper. Serve with favorite condiments.

Makes 4 servings

Tip: For zesty flavor, top sandwiches with pickled peppers and a dollop of mustard.

Barbecued Pulled Pork

Cook Time: 8 to 10 hours

1 boneless pork shoulder or butt roast (3 to 4 pounds)

1 teaspoon salt

1 teaspoon ground cumin

1 teaspoon paprika

1 teaspoon black pepper

½ teaspoon ground red pepper

1 medium onion, thinly sliced

1 medium green bell pepper, cut into strips

1 bottle (18 ounces) barbecue sauce

½ cup packed light brown sugar

Sandwich rolls or hot cooked rice

1. Trim excess fat from pork. Combine salt, cumin, paprika, black pepper and red pepper in small bowl; rub over roast.

2. Place onion and bell pepper in 5-quart slow cooker; add pork. Combine barbecue sauce and brown sugar in medium bowl; pour over meat. Cover; cook on LOW 8 to 10 hours.

3. Transfer roast to cutting board. Trim and discard remaining fat from roast. Pull pork into coarse shreds using 2 forks. Serve pork with sauce on sandwich rolls or over rice.

Makes 4 to 6 servings

Shredded Beef Wraps

Prep Time: 10 minutes   **Cook Time:** 7 to 8 hours

1 beef flank steak or beef skirt steak (1 to 1½ pounds)

1 cup beef broth

½ cup sun-dried tomatoes (not packed in oil), chopped

3 to 4 cloves garlic, minced

¼ teaspoon ground cumin

8 flour tortillas

Toppings: Shredded lettuce, diced tomatoes and shredded Monterey Jack cheese

1. Cut flank steak into quarters. Place flank steak, beef broth, tomatoes, garlic and cumin in slow cooker. Cover; cook on LOW 7 to 8 hours or until meat is tender.

2. Remove beef from slow cooker; shred beef with 2 forks or cut into thin strips.

3. Place remaining juices from slow cooker in blender or food processor; blend until sauce is smooth.

4. Spoon meat onto tortillas with small amount of sauce. Add desired toppings. Roll up and serve.

Makes 4 servings

Hot & Juicy Reuben Sandwiches

Prep Time: 25 minutes   **Cook Time:** 7 to 9 hours

1 mild-cure corned beef (about
   1½ pounds)

2 cups sauerkraut, drained

½ cup beef broth

1 small onion, sliced

1 clove garlic, minced

¼ teaspoon caraway seeds

4 to 6 peppercorns

8 slices pumpernickel or rye
   bread

4 slices Swiss cheese

   Mustard

1. Trim excess fat from corned beef. Place meat in slow cooker. Add sauerkraut, broth, onion, garlic, caraway seeds and peppercorns.

2. Cover; cook on LOW 7 to 9 hours.

3. Remove beef from slow cooker. Cut across the grain into ¼-inch-thick slices. Divide evenly on 4 slices bread. Top each slice with ½ cup drained sauerkraut mixture and one slice cheese. Spread mustard on remaining 4 bread slices. Close sandwich.

Makes 4 servings

Note: This two-fisted stack of corned beef, sauerkraut and melted Swiss cheese makes a glorious sandwich you'll serve often using slow-cooked corned beef.

Italian-Style Shredded Beef

Prep Time: 10 minutes   **Cook Time:** 6 hours (HIGH)

1 (2½-pound) boneless eye of
   round beef roast

1 medium onion, thinly sliced

1 (6-ounce) can Italian flavored
   tomato paste

6 teaspoons HERB-OX® beef
   flavored bouillon

½ cup water

12 Kaiser rolls

12 (1-ounce) slices Provolone
   cheese

Place roast in 3½-quart slow cooker. Add onion and remaining ingredients except rolls and cheese. Cover and cook on HIGH for 5 to 6 hours or until meat is tender. Remove roast from cooker. Using two forks, shred meat. Return meat to cooker; stirring to coat with sauce. Evenly divide meat among Kaiser rolls. Top with cheese and serve.

Makes 12 servings

Shredded Apricot Pork Sandwiches

Cook Time: 8¼ to 9½ hours

2 medium onions, thinly sliced

1 cup apricot preserves

½ cup packed dark brown sugar

½ cup barbecue sauce

¼ cup cider vinegar

2 tablespoons Worcestershire sauce

½ teaspoon red pepper flakes

1 (4-pound) boneless pork top loin roast, trimmed of fat

¼ cup cold water

2 tablespoons cornstarch

1 tablespoon grated fresh ginger

1 teaspoon salt

1 teaspoon black pepper

10 to 12 sesame or onion rolls, toasted

1. Combine onions, preserves, brown sugar, barbecue sauce, vinegar, Worcestershire sauce and pepper flakes in small bowl. Place pork roast in 5-quart slow cooker. Pour apricot mixture over roast. Cover; cook on LOW 8 to 9 hours.

2. Transfer pork to cutting board; cool slightly. Shred pork into coarse shreds using 2 forks. Let cooking liquid stand 5 minutes to allow fat to rise. Skim fat.

3. Blend water, cornstarch, ginger, salt and pepper until smooth. Whisk cornstarch mixture into cooking liquid. Cook, uncovered, on HIGH 15 to 30 minutes or until thickened. Return shredded pork to slow cooker; mix well. Serve on toasted buns.

Makes 10 to 12 sandwiches

Variation: A 4-pound pork shoulder roast, cut into pieces and trimmed of fat, can be substituted for pork loin roast.

Barbecued Beef Sandwiches

Prep Time: 20 to 25 minutes   **Cook Time:** 8¼ to 10¼ hours

3 pounds boneless beef chuck
    shoulder roast

2 cups ketchup

1 medium onion, chopped

¼ cup cider vinegar

¼ cup dark molasses

2 tablespoons Worcestershire
    sauce

2 cloves garlic, minced

½ teaspoon salt

½ teaspoon dry mustard

½ teaspoon black pepper

¼ teaspoon garlic powder

¼ teaspoon red pepper flakes
    Sesame seed buns, split

1. Cut roast in half; place in 4- to 5-quart slow cooker. Combine ketchup, onion, vinegar, molasses, Worcestershire sauce, garlic, salt, mustard, black pepper, garlic powder and red pepper flakes in large bowl. Pour sauce mixture over roast. Cover; cook on LOW 8 to 10 hours or on HIGH 4 to 5 hours.

2. Remove roast from sauce; cool slightly. Trim and discard excess fat from beef. Shred meat using two forks.

3. Let sauce stand 5 minutes to allow fat to rise. Skim off fat.

4. Return shredded meat to slow cooker. Stir meat to evenly coat with sauce. Adjust seasonings. Cover; cook 15 to 30 minutes or until hot.

5. Spoon filling into sandwich buns and top with additional sauce, if desired.

Makes 12 servings

Tex-Mex Beef Wraps

Cook Time: 8 to 9 hours

1 tablespoon chili powder

2 teaspoons ground cumin

1 teaspoon salt

¼ teaspoon ground red pepper

1 boneless beef chuck pot roast (2½ to 3 pounds), cut into 4 pieces

1 medium onion, chopped

3 cloves garlic, minced

1 cup salsa, divided

12 flour or corn tortillas (6 to 7 inches), warmed

1 cup shredded Cheddar or Monterey Jack cheese

1 cup chopped tomato

1 ripe avocado, diced

¼ cup chopped cilantro

1. Coat slow cooker with cooking spray. Blend chili powder, cumin, salt and red pepper. Rub meat all over with spice mixture. Place onion and garlic in bottom of 3½-quart slow cooker; top with meat. Spoon ½ cup salsa over meat. Cover and cook on LOW 8 to 9 hours or on HIGH 3½ to 4½ hours, or until meat is very tender.

2. Remove meat from slow cooker; place on plate and use 2 forks to shred meat. Skim off and discard fat from juices in slow cooker; return meat to juices and mix well. Place meat on warm tortillas, top with cheese, tomato, avocado and cilantro; roll up wrap. Serve with remaining salsa. *Makes 6 servings*

Barbecue Pork on Buns

Cook Time: 5 to 6 hours (HIGH)

1 (2-pound) boneless pork loin

1 onion, chopped

¾ cup cola-flavored carbonated beverage

¾ cup barbecue sauce

8 sandwich buns

Combine all ingredients except buns in a 4-quart slow cooker; cook, covered, on HIGH for 5 to 6 hours or until very tender. Drain; slice or shred pork. Serve on buns with additional barbecue sauce, if desired.

Makes 8 servings

Tip: Pork can be made 1 to 2 days ahead; refrigerate covered and reheat before serving.

Favorite recipe from **National Pork Board**

Hot Beef Sandwiches

Cook Time: 8 to 10 hours

1 chuck beef roast (3 to 4 pounds), cut into chunks

1 jar (6 ounces) sliced dill pickles, undrained

1 can (14 ounces) crushed tomatoes with Italian seasoning

1 medium onion, diced

4 cloves garlic, minced

1 teaspoon mustard seeds

Hamburger buns

1. Place beef in 5-quart slow cooker. Pour pickles with juice over top of beef. Add tomatoes, onion, garlic and mustard seeds.

2. Cover; cook on LOW 8 to 10 hours.

3. Remove beef from slow cooker. Shred beef with two forks. Return beef to tomato mixture; mix well. Serve beef mixture on buns. *Makes 6 to 8 servings*

Tip: Pile this beef onto a toasted roll or bun and you'll have an out-of-this world sandwich! Serve with lettuce, sliced tomatoes, red onion slices or shredded slaw.

Burgundy Beef Po' Boys with Dipping Sauce

Cook Time: 8 to 10 hours

1 boneless beef chuck shoulder or bottom round roast (3 pounds)

2 cups chopped onions

¼ cup red wine

3 tablespoons balsamic vinegar

1 tablespoon beef bouillon granules

1 tablespoon Worcestershire sauce

¾ teaspoon dried thyme

½ teaspoon garlic powder

Italian rolls, warmed and split

1. Cut beef into 3 or 4 pieces; trim fat. Place onions on bottom of 4- to 5-quart slow cooker. Top with beef and remaining ingredients except rolls. Cover; cook on LOW 8 to 10 hours or until beef is very tender.

2. Remove beef from cooking liquid; cool slightly. Trim and discard fat from beef. Using two forks, shred meat. Let cooking liquid stand 5 minutes to allow fat to rise. Skim off fat.

3. Spoon beef into rolls and serve liquid as dipping sauce. *Makes 6 to 8 sandwiches*

Super Sides

South-of-the-Border Macaroni & Cheese

Prep Time: 15 minutes   **Cook Time:** 2 hours (HIGH)

5 cups cooked rotini pasta

2 cups (8 ounces) cubed American cheese

1 can (12 ounces) evaporated milk

1 cup (4 ounces) cubed sharp Cheddar cheese

1 can (4 ounces) diced green chilies, drained

2 teaspoons chili powder

2 medium tomatoes, seeded and chopped

5 green onions, sliced

1. Combine all ingredients, except tomatoes and onions in slow cooker; mix well. Cover; cook on HIGH 2 hours, stirring twice.

2. Stir in tomatoes and green onions; continue cooking until hot.   *Makes 4 servings*

Layered Mexican-Style Casserole

Prep Time: 15 minutes   **Cook Time:** 6 to 8 hours

2 cans (15½ ounces each)
    hominy,* drained

1 can (15 ounces) black beans,
    rinsed and drained

1 can (14½ ounces) diced
    tomatoes with garlic, basil
    and oregano, undrained

1 cup thick and chunky salsa

1 can (6 ounces) tomato paste

½ teaspoon ground cumin

3 (9-inch) flour tortillas

2 cups (8 ounces) shredded
    Monterey Jack cheese

¼ cup sliced black olives

*Hominy is corn that has been treated
to remove the germ and hull. It can be
found with the canned vegetables or
beans in most supermarkets.*

1. Prepare foil handles (see below). Spray slow cooker with nonstick cooking spray.

2. Combine hominy, beans, tomatoes with juice, salsa, tomato paste and cumin in bowl.

3. Press one tortilla in bottom of slow cooker. (Edges of tortilla may turn up slightly.) Top with one third of hominy mixture and one third of cheese. Repeat layers. Press remaining tortilla on top. Top with remaining hominy mixture. Set aside remaining cheese.

4. Cover; cook on LOW 6 to 8 hours. Sprinkle with remaining cheese and olives. Cover; let stand 5 minutes. Pull out tortilla stack with foil handles.   *Makes 6 servings*

Foil Handles: Tear off three 18×2-inch strips of heavy-duty foil or use regular foil folded to double thickness. Crisscross foil strips in spoke design and place into slow cooker to make lifting of tortilla stack easier.

Chunky Vanilla Pears

Cook Time: 1 hour (HIGH)

1¼ pounds ripe pears, peeled and
    diced

8 dried orange essence plums,
    cut into quarters

¼ cup granulated sugar

1 tablespoon lemon juice

½ teaspoon vanilla

1. Combine all ingredients, except vanilla in 1½-quart slow cooker. Cover; cook 1 hour on HIGH.

2. Stir in vanilla. Serve hot or at room temperature with roasted ham, pork or chicken. Or, serve as a dessert sauce over ice cream or pound cake.   *Makes 2 cups*

Risotto-Style Peppered Rice

Cook Time: 4 to 5 hours

1 cup uncooked converted long grain rice

1 medium green bell pepper, chopped

1 medium red bell pepper, chopped

1 cup chopped onion

½ teaspoon ground turmeric

⅛ teaspoon ground red pepper (optional)

1 can (14½ ounces) fat-free chicken broth

4 ounces Monterey Jack cheese with jalapeño peppers, cubed

½ cup milk

¼ cup (½ stick) butter, cubed

1 teaspoon salt

1. Place rice, bell peppers, onion, turmeric and ground red pepper, if desired, in slow cooker. Stir in broth.

2. Cover; cook on LOW 4 to 5 hours or until rice is tender.

3. Stir in cheese, milk, butter and salt; fluff rice with fork. Cover; cook on LOW 5 minutes or until cheese melts.

Makes 4 to 6 servings

Easy Dirty Rice

Cook Time: 2 hours

½ pound bulk Italian sausage

2 cups water

1 cup uncooked long grain rice

1 large onion, finely chopped

1 large green bell pepper, finely chopped

½ cup finely chopped celery

1½ teaspoons salt

½ teaspoon ground red pepper

½ cup chopped fresh parsley

1. Brown sausage in skillet over medium-high heat, stirring to break up meat. Place sausage into slow cooker.

2. Stir in all remaining ingredients except parsley. Cover; cook on LOW 2 hours or until rice is tender. Stir in parsley.

Makes 4 servings

Orange-Spice Glazed Carrots

Cook Time: 3½ to 4 hours

1 package (32 ounces) baby carrots

½ cup packed light brown sugar

½ cup orange juice

3 tablespoons butter or margarine

¾ teaspoon ground cinnamon

¼ teaspoon ground nutmeg

¼ cup cold water

2 tablespoons cornstarch

1. Combine all ingredients except cornstarch and water in slow cooker. Cover and cook on LOW 3½ to 4 hours or until carrots are crisp-tender. Spoon carrots into serving bowl.

2. Transfer juices to small saucepan; bring to a boil. Mix water and cornstarch in small bowl until smooth. Stir into saucepan. Boil 1 minute or until thickened, stirring constantly. Spoon over carrots.

Makes 6 servings

Mama's Best Baked Beans

Cook Time: 2 to 4 hours

1 bag (1 pound) dried Great Northern beans

1 package (1 pound) bacon

5 hot dogs, cut into ½-inch pieces

1 cup chopped onion

1 bottle (24 ounces) ketchup

2 cups dark brown sugar

1. Soak and cook beans according to package directions. Drain and refrigerate until ready to use.

2. Cook bacon in a skillet over medium-high heat until crisp. Drain on paper towels. Crumble bacon and set aside. Discard all but 3 tablespoons bacon fat from skillet. Add hot dogs and onion. Cook and stir over medium heat until onion is tender.

3. Combine cooked beans, bacon, hot dog mixture, ketchup and brown sugar in slow cooker.

4. Cover; cook on LOW 2 to 4 hours.

Makes 4 servings

Eggplant Italiano

Prep Time: 10 minutes   **Cook Time:** 4¼ to 5 hours

1¼ **pounds eggplant, cut into 1-inch cubes**

2 **medium onions, thinly sliced**

2 **ribs celery, cut into 1-inch pieces**

1 **can (16 ounces) diced tomatoes, undrained**

3 **tablespoons tomato sauce**

1 **tablespoon olive oil, divided**

½ **cup pitted ripe olives, cut in half**

2 **tablespoons balsamic vinegar**

1 **tablespoon sugar**

1 **tablespoon capers, rinsed and drained**

1 **teaspoon dried oregano or basil**

Salt and black pepper

1. Combine eggplant, onions, celery, tomatoes with juice, tomato sauce and oil in slow cooker. Cover and cook on LOW 3½ to 4 hours or until eggplant is tender.

2. Stir in olives, vinegar, sugar, capers and oregano. Season with salt and pepper to taste. Cover and cook 45 minutes to 1 hour or until heated through.   *Makes 6 servings*

Tip: Balsamic vinegar is made from sweet white grapes. Because it is aged for many years to develop its characteristic mellow flavor, it is expensive. Any wine vinegar can be substituted for it.

Blue Cheese Potatoes

Cook Time: 7 hours

2 pounds red potatoes, peeled and cut into ½-inch pieces

1¼ cups chopped green onions, divided

2 tablespoons olive oil, divided

1 teaspoon dried basil

½ teaspoon salt

¼ teaspoon black pepper

2 ounces crumbled blue cheese

1. Layer potatoes, 1 cup onions, 1 tablespoon oil, basil, salt and pepper in slow cooker. Cover; cook on LOW 7 hours or on HIGH 4 hours.

2. Gently stir in cheese and remaining 1 tablespoon oil. If slow cooker is on LOW turn to HIGH; cook an additional 5 minutes to allow flavors to blend. Transfer potatoes to serving platter and top with remaining ¼ cup onions.

Makes 5 servings

Slow Cooker Cheddar Polenta

Cook Time: 2 hours (HIGH)

7 cups hot water

2 cups polenta (not "quick-cooking") or coarse-ground yellow cornmeal

2 tablespoons extra-virgin olive oil

2 teaspoons salt

3 cups grated CABOT® Extra Sharp or Sharp Cheddar (about 12 ounces)

1. Combine water, polenta, olive oil and salt in slow cooker; whisk until well blended. Add cheese and whisk again.

2. Cover and cook on HIGH setting for 2 hours or until liquid is mostly absorbed. Stir together well. (Polenta should have consistency of thick cooked cereal.)

Makes 8 servings

Note: If not serving polenta right away, pour it onto an oiled baking sheet with sides, spreading into an even layer; cover with plastic wrap and let it cool. When ready to serve, cut polenta into rectangles and sauté it in nonstick skillet with olive oil until golden on both sides.

Risi Bisi

Cook Time: 3 to 4 hours

1½ cups converted long-grain white rice

¾ cup chopped onion

2 cloves garlic, minced

2 cans (about 14 ounces each) reduced-sodium chicken broth

⅓ cup water

¾ teaspoon Italian seasoning

½ teaspoon dried basil

½ cup frozen peas, thawed

¼ cup grated Parmesan cheese

¼ cup toasted pine nuts (optional)

1. Combine rice, onion and garlic in slow cooker. Bring broth and water to a boil in small saucepan. Stir broth mixture, Italian seasoning and basil into rice mixture. Cover; cook on LOW 2 to 3 hours or until liquid is absorbed.

2. Add peas. Cover; cook 1 hour. Stir in cheese. Spoon rice into serving bowl. Sprinkle with pine nuts, if desired.

Makes 6 servings

Polenta-Style Corn Casserole

Cook Time: 4¼ to 5½

1 can (14½ ounces) chicken broth

½ cup cornmeal

1 can (7 ounces) corn, drained

1 can (4 ounces) mild green chilies, drained

¼ cup diced red bell pepper

½ teaspoon salt

¼ teaspoon black pepper

1 cup (4 ounces) shredded Cheddar cheese

1. Pour chicken broth into slow cooker. Whisk in cornmeal. Add corn, chilies, bell pepper, salt and black pepper. Cover; cook on LOW 4 to 5 hours or on HIGH 2 to 3 hours.

2. Stir in cheese. Continue cooking, uncovered, 15 to 30 minutes or until cheese melts.

Makes 6 servings

Serving Suggestion: Divide cooked corn mixture into lightly greased individual ramekins or spread in pie plate; cover and refrigerate. Serve at room temperature or warm in oven or microwave.

Mexican-Style Rice and Cheese

Cook Time: 6 to 8 hours

1 can (15 ounces) Mexican-style
beans

1 can (14½ ounces) diced
tomatoes with jalapeños,
undrained

2 cups (8 ounces) shredded
Monterey Jack or Colby
cheese, divided

1½ cups uncooked long-grain
converted rice

1 large onion, finely chopped

½ package (4 ounces) cream
cheese

3 cloves garlic, minced

1. Grease inside of slow cooker well.
Combine beans, tomatoes with juice, 1 cup
cheese, rice, onion, cream cheese and garlic
in slow cooker; mix well.

2. Cover; cook on LOW 6 to 8 hours.

3. Sprinkle with remaining 1 cup cheese just
before serving.   *Makes 6 to 8 servings*

Easy Holiday Stuffing

Prep Time: 10 minutes   **Total Time:** 3¾ to 6¾ hours

1 cup butter, melted

2 cups chopped celery

1 cup chopped onion

1 teaspoon poultry seasoning

1 teaspoon leaf sage, crumbled

½ teaspoon ground black pepper

3 tablespoons HERB-OX®
chicken flavored bouillon

2 eggs, beaten

2 cups water

12 cups dry breadcrumbs

In large bowl, combine butter, celery, onion,
seasonings, bouillon, eggs and water
together. Add breadcrumbs and stir to blend.
Place mixture in 5-quart slow cooker. Cook
on HIGH for 45 minutes; reduce heat to
LOW and cook for 6 hours or cook on HIGH
for 3 hours.   *Makes 12 servings*

Hearty Entrées

Chipotle Taco Filling

Cook Time: 4 hours

2 pounds ground beef

2 cups chopped onions

2 cans (15 ounces each) pinto beans, rinsed and drained

1 can (14½ ounces) diced tomatoes with peppers and onions, drained

2 chipotle peppers in adobo sauce, mashed

1 tablespoon beef bouillon granules

1 tablespoon sugar

1½ teaspoons ground cumin

Taco shells or flour tortillas

Shredded lettuce, salsa, shredded Mexican blend cheese and sour cream (optional)

1. Brown ground beef in large nonstick skillet over medium-high heat, stirring to separate meat. Drain fat.

2. Combine beef, onions, beans, tomatoes, peppers, bouillon, sugar and cumin in 3-quart slow cooker. Cover; cook on LOW 4 hours or on HIGH 2 hours.

3. Serve filling in taco shells. Top with lettuce, salsa, cheese and sour cream, if desired.

Makes 8 cups filling

Sweet and Sour Shrimp

Prep Time: 15 to 20 minutes   **Cook Time:** 3½ to 4½ hours

1 can (16 ounces) sliced peaches in syrup, undrained

½ cup chopped green onions

½ cup chopped red bell pepper

½ cup chopped green bell pepper

½ cup chopped celery

⅓ cup vegetable broth

¼ cup light soy sauce

2 tablespoons rice wine vinegar

2 tablespoons dark sesame oil

1 teaspoon red pepper flakes

6 ounces snow peas

1 pound cooked medium shrimp

1 cup cherry tomatoes, cut into halves

½ cup toasted walnut pieces

1. Place peaches, onions, bell peppers, celery, broth, soy sauce, vinegar, sesame oil, and red pepper flakes in slow cooker. Cover; cook on LOW 3 to 4 hours or on HIGH 2 to 3 hours or until vegetables are tender. Stir well.

2. Add snow peas. Cook 15 minutes on HIGH. Add shrimp, tomatoes and walnuts. Cook 4 to 5 minutes on HIGH or until shrimp is hot. Serve with rice.

Makes 4 to 6 servings

Arroz con Pollo

Prep Time: 10 minutes   **Cook Time:** 6 to 8 hours

6 chicken thighs, skin removed

1 can (14½ ounces) chicken broth

1 can (14½ ounces) stewed tomatoes

1 package (10 ounces) frozen peas

1 package (8 ounces) Spanish-style yellow rice mix

1½ cups *French's*® French Fried Onions, divided

1. Coat slow cooker with vegetable cooking spray. Combine chicken, broth and tomatoes in slow cooker. Cover and cook on LOW setting for 4 to 5 hours (or on HIGH for 2 to 2½ hours) until chicken is fork-tender.

2. Stir in peas and rice mix. Cover and cook on LOW setting for 2 to 3 hours (or on HIGH for 1 to 1½ hours) until rice is cooked and all liquid is absorbed. Stir in ¾ *cup* French Fried Onions. Spoon soup into serving bowls; top with remaining onions.

Makes 6 servings

Turkey Chili

Prep Time: 30 minutes   **Cook Time:** 4 hours

20 ounces JENNIE-O TURKEY STORE® Extra Lean Ground Turkey Breast

1 cup diced onions

1 (10-ounce) package shredded carrots

2 green bell peppers, diced

2 zucchini, diced

2 yellow squash, diced

6 cups water

2 tablespoons HERB-OX® Beef Bouillon Granules

1 (28-ounce) can diced tomatoes

1 (24-ounce) jar salsa

1 (15-ounce) can black beans, drained and rinsed

1 (15-ounce) can kidney beans, drained and rinsed

2 tablespoons chili powder

Brown and crumble ground turkey in large nonstick pan coated with vegetable spray over medium-high heat. Add vegetables to pan and cook for about 5 minutes or until onions are tender. Place turkey and vegetables in 6½-quart slow cooker along with water, beef granules, diced tomatoes, salsa, beans and chili powder. Cover and cook mixture on LOW setting for 4 hours.

Makes 20 servings

Veggie Mac and Tuna

Cook Time: 2½ hours

1½ cups (6 ounces) elbow macaroni

3 tablespoons butter or margarine

1 small onion, chopped

½ medium red bell pepper, chopped

½ medium green bell pepper, chopped

¼ cup all-purpose flour

1¾ cups milk

8 ounces cubed light pasteurized process cheese product

½ teaspoon dried marjoram

1 package (10 ounces) frozen peas, thawed

1 can (9 ounces) tuna in water, drained

1. Cook macaroni according to package directions until just tender; drain.

2. Melt butter in medium saucepan over medium heat. Add onion and bell peppers. Cook and stir 5 minutes or until tender. Add flour. Stir constantly 2 minutes over medium heat. Stir in milk. Bring to a boil. Boil, stirring constantly, until thickened. Reduce heat to low; add cheese and marjoram. Stir until cheese is melted.

3. Combine macaroni, cheese sauce, peas and tuna in slow cooker. Cover and cook on LOW 2½ hours or until bubbly at edge.

Makes 6 servings

Swiss Steak Stew

Cook Time: 8 hours

2 to 3 boneless beef top sirloin steaks (about 4 pounds)

2 cans (14½ ounces each) diced tomatoes, undrained

2 green bell peppers, sliced into ½-inch strips

2 medium onions, chopped

1 tablespoon seasoned salt

1 teaspoon seasoned pepper

1. Cut each steak into 3 to 4 pieces. Place steaks in 5-quart slow cooker. Add tomatoes with juice, bell peppers and onions. Sprinkle with salt and pepper.

2. Cover; cook on LOW 8 hours or until meat is tender.

Makes 10 servings

Caribbean Sweet Potato & Bean Stew

Prep Time: 10 minutes   **Cook Time:** 5 to 6 hours

2 medium sweet potatoes (about 1 pound), peeled and cut into 1-inch cubes

2 cups frozen cut green beans, thawed

1 can (15 ounces) black beans, rinsed and drained

1 can (14½ ounces) vegetable broth

1 small onion, sliced

2 teaspoons Caribbean jerk seasoning

½ teaspoon dried thyme

¼ teaspoon salt

¼ teaspoon ground cinnamon

⅓ cup slivered almonds, toasted*

Hot pepper sauce (optional)

To toast almonds, spread in single layer on baking sheet. Bake in preheated 350°F oven 8 to 10 minutes or until golden brown, stirring frequently.

1. Combine sweet potatoes, beans, broth, onion, jerk seasoning, thyme, salt and cinnamon in slow cooker.

2. Cover; cook on LOW 5 to 6 hours or until vegetables are tender.

3. Adjust seasonings. Serve with almonds and hot pepper sauce, if desired.

Makes 4 servings

Shredded Beef Fajitas

Cook Time: 8 to 10 hours

1 beef flank steak (about
    1½ pounds)

1 can (14½ ounces) diced
    tomatoes with jalapeños,
    undrained

1 cup chopped onion

1 medium green bell pepper, cut
    into ½-inch pieces

2 cloves garlic, minced *or*
    ¼ teaspoon garlic powder

1 package (1½ ounces) fajita
    seasoning mix

12 (8-inch) flour tortillas

Toppings: sour cream,
    guacamole, shredded
    Cheddar cheese, salsa
    (optional)

1. Cut flank steak into 6 portions; place in slow cooker. Combine tomatoes with juice, onion, bell pepper, garlic and fajita seasoning mix; pour over meat. Cover; cook on LOW 8 to 10 hours or on HIGH 4 to 5 hours.

2. Remove beef from slow cooker; shred. Return beef to slow cooker and stir.

3. To serve fajitas, place meat mixture evenly into flour tortillas. Add toppings as desired; roll up tortillas.   *Makes 12 servings*

Iron Range Pot Roast

Cook Time: 8 to 9 hours

1 (3-pound) boneless pork
    shoulder (Boston Butt) roast

2 teaspoons Italian seasoning

1 teaspoon fennel seeds,
    crushed

1 teaspoon salt

½ teaspoon celery seeds

½ teaspoon ground black pepper

Vegetable oil

2 large potatoes, peeled and cut
    into ¾-inch slices

4 garlic cloves, sliced

¾ cup beef broth (or water)

Mix together seasonings and rub over all surfaces of pork roast. Brown roast in a little oil in large skillet over medium-high heat, turning often to brown evenly. Place potatoes and garlic in 3½- to 4-quart slow cooker; pour broth over and top with browned pork roast. Cover and cook on LOW for 8 to 9 hours, until pork is very tender. Slice pork and serve with vegetables and juices.

Makes 6 to 8 servings

Favorite recipe from **National Pork Board**

Beef with Apples & Sweet Potatoes

Prep Time: 20 minutes   **Cook Time:** 8¼ to 9¼ hours

1 boneless beef chuck shoulder
   roast (2 pounds)

1 can (40 ounces) sweet
   potatoes, drained

2 small onions, sliced

2 apples, cored and sliced

½ cup beef broth

2 cloves garlic, minced

1 teaspoon salt

1 teaspoon dried thyme, divided

¾ teaspoon black pepper,
   divided

1 tablespoon cornstarch

¼ teaspoon ground cinnamon

2 tablespoons cold water

1. Trim fat from beef and cut into 2-inch pieces. Place beef, sweet potatoes, onions, apples, beef broth, garlic, salt, ½ teaspoon thyme and ½ teaspoon pepper in 3½- to 4-quart slow cooker. Cover; cook on LOW 8 to 9 hours or until beef is tender.

2. Transfer beef, sweet potatoes and apples to platter; keep warm. Let liquid stand 5 minutes to allow fat to rise. Skim off fat.

3. Combine cornstarch, remaining ½ teaspoon thyme, ¼ teaspoon pepper, cinnamon and water until smooth; stir into cooking liquid. Cook 15 minutes or until juices are thickened. Serve sauce with beef, sweet potatoes and apples.   *Makes 6 servings*

Sweet & Saucy Ribs

Prep Time: 10 minutes   **Cook Time:** 6 to 8 hours

2 pounds pork baby back ribs

1 teaspoon black pepper

2½ cups barbecue sauce (not mesquite flavored)

1 jar (8 ounces) cherry jam or preserves

1 tablespoon Dijon mustard

¼ teaspoon salt

Additional salt and black pepper (optional)

1. Trim excess fat from ribs. Rub 1 teaspoon pepper over ribs. Cut ribs into 2-rib portions; place in slow cooker.

2. Combine barbecue sauce, jam, mustard and ¼ teaspoon salt in small bowl; pour over ribs.

3. Cover; cook on LOW 6 to 8 hours or until ribs are tender. Season with additional salt and pepper, if desired. Serve ribs with sauce.

Makes 4 servings

Black Bean and Turkey Stew

Cook Time: 6¼ to 8¼ hours

3 cans (15 ounces each) black beans, rinsed and drained

1½ cups chopped onions

1 can (14½ ounces) fat-free reduced-sodium chicken broth

1 cup sliced celery

1 cup chopped red bell pepper

4 cloves garlic, minced

1½ teaspoons dried oregano

¾ teaspoon ground coriander

½ teaspoon ground cumin

¼ teaspoon ground red pepper

6 ounces cooked turkey sausage, thinly sliced

1. Combine all ingredients, except sausage, in slow cooker. Cover; cook on LOW 6 to 8 hours.

2. Transfer about 1½ cups bean mixture from slow cooker to blender or food processor; purée bean mixture. Return to slow cooker. Stir in sausage. Cover; cook on LOW an additional 10 to 15 minutes.

Makes 6 servings

Three Pepper Pasta Sauce

Prep Time: 10 to 15 minutes   **Cook Time:** 7 to 8 hours

1 *each* red, yellow and green
    bell pepper, cut into 1-inch
    pieces

2 cans (14½ ounces each) diced
    tomatoes, undrained

1 cup chopped onion

1 can (6 ounces) tomato paste

4 cloves garlic, minced

2 tablespoons olive oil

1 teaspoon dried basil

1 teaspoon dried oregano

½ teaspoon salt

¼ teaspoon red pepper flakes or
    ground black pepper

    Hot cooked pasta

    Shredded Parmesan or
    Romano cheese

1. Combine bell peppers, tomatoes with juice, onion, tomato paste, garlic, olive oil, basil, oregano, salt and red pepper flakes in slow cooker. Cover; cook on LOW 7 to 8 hours or until vegetables are tender.

2. Adjust seasonings, if desired. Serve with pasta and cheese.   *Makes 4 to 6 servings*

Tip: You can substitute 3 cups mixed bell pepper chunks from a salad bar for the peppers.

Italian-Style Sausage with Rice

Prep Time: 10 to 15 minutes   **Cook Time:** 4 to 6 hours

1 pound mild Italian sausage links, cut into 1-inch pieces

1 can (15 ounces) pinto beans, rinsed and drained

1 cup pasta sauce

1 green bell pepper, cut into strips

1 small onion, halved and sliced

½ teaspoon salt

¼ teaspoon black pepper

Hot cooked rice

Chopped fresh basil (optional)

1. Brown sausage in large nonstick skillet over medium heat. Drain and discard fat.

2. Place sausage, beans, pasta sauce, bell pepper, onion, salt and black pepper into slow cooker. Cover; cook on LOW 4 to 6 hours.

3. Serve with rice. Garnish with basil, if desired.

Makes 4 to 5 servings

Cajun Beef Stew

Cook Time: 7½ to 8½ hours

1 tablespoon Cajun or blackened seasoning mix

1 pound beef stew meat (1½-inch chunks)

1 pound red potatoes, cut into 1½-inch chunks

1 medium onion, cut into thin wedges

1½ cups baby carrots

1 can (14½ ounces) beef broth

3 tablespoons cornstarch

3 tablespoons water

Salt

Chopped parsley or thyme (optional)

1. Sprinkle seasoning mix over meat. Place potatoes, onion and carrots in bottom of slow cooker. Place meat on top of vegetables. Add broth. Cover and cook on LOW 7 to 8 hours or on HIGH 4 to 5 hours or until beef and vegetables are tender.

2. With slotted spoon, transfer beef and vegetables to serving bowl; cover with foil to keep warm. Turn slow cooker to HIGH. Combine cornstarch with water until smooth. Stir into juices; cover and cook 15 to 20 minutes or until thickened. Season to taste with salt. Spoon sauce over beef and vegetables. Transfer to shallow bowls to serve; garnish as desired. *Makes 4 servings*

Meatballs in Burgundy Sauce

Cook Time: 4 to 5 hours (HIGH)

60 frozen prepared fully-cooked meatballs, partially thawed and separated

3 cups chopped onions

1½ cups water

1 cup red wine

2 packages (about 1 ounce each) beef gravy mix

¼ cup ketchup

1 tablespoon dried oregano

1 package (8 ounces) curly noodles

1. Combine meatballs, onions, water, wine, gravy mix, ketchup and oregano in slow cooker; stir to blend.

2. Cover; cook on HIGH 4 to 5 hours.

3. Meanwhile, cook noodles according to package directions. Serve meatballs with noodles. *Makes 6 to 8 servings*

Serving Suggestion: Serve meatballs as an appetizer with remaining sauce as a dip.

Lemon-Thyme Beef with Beans

Prep Time: 20 minutes   **Cook Time:** 8 to 9 hours

1 beef chuck roast (about 3 pounds), trimmed and cut into 2-inch pieces

2 cans (15 ounces each) white or pinto beans, rinsed and drained

1 can (15 ounces) red kidney beans, rinsed and drained

1 cup beef broth

1 medium onion, chopped

2 cloves garlic, minced

1 teaspoon salt

1 teaspoon grated lemon peel

1 teaspoon dried thyme

1 teaspoon black pepper

Chopped fresh parsley

1. Place all ingredients, except parsley, in slow cooker. Cover; cook on LOW 8 to 9 hours or until beef is tender.

2. Adjust seasonings before serving, if desired. Arrange beef on top of beans. Garnish with parsley. *Makes 6 to 8 servings*

Easy Desserts

Baked Ginger Apples

Cook Time: 4½ hours

4 large Red Delicious apples

½ cup (1 stick) unsalted butter, melted

⅓ cup chopped macadamia nuts

¼ cup chopped dried apricots

2 tablespoons finely chopped crystallized ginger

1 tablespoon dark brown sugar

¾ cup brandy

½ cup vanilla pudding and pie filling mix

2 cups heavy cream

1. Slice tops off apples; core. Combine butter, nuts, apricots, ginger and brown sugar in medium bowl. Fill apples with nut mixture. Place apples in slow cooker. Pour brandy into slow cooker. Cover; cook on LOW 4 hours or on HIGH 2 hours.

2. Gently remove apples from slow cooker; keep warm. Combine pudding mix and cream in small bowl. Add to slow cooker; mix well. Cover; cook on HIGH 30 minutes. Stir until smooth. Return apples to slow cooker; keep warm until ready to serve.

3. Serve apples with cream mixture.

Makes 4 servings

Baked Fudge Pudding Cake

Cook Time: 3 to 4 hours

6 tablespoons unsweetened cocoa powder

¼ cup all-purpose flour

⅛ teaspoon salt

4 eggs

1⅓ cups sugar

1 cup (2 sticks) unsalted butter, melted

1 teaspoon vanilla

Grated peel of 1 orange

½ cup whipping cream

Chopped toasted pecans, whipped cream or vanilla ice cream

1. Spray inside of slow cooker with nonstick cooking spray. Preheat slow cooker on LOW setting. Combine cocoa, flour and salt in small bowl; set aside.

2. Beat eggs with electric mixer on medium-high speed until thickened. Gradually add sugar; beat 5 minutes or until very thick and lemon-colored. Mix in butter, vanilla and peel. Stir cocoa mixture into egg mixture. Add cream; mix until blended. Pour batter into slow cooker.

3. Before placing lid on slow cooker, cover opening with paper towel to collect condensation, making sure it doesn't touch pudding mixture. (Large slow cookers might require 2 connected paper towels.) Place lid over paper towel. Cook on LOW 3 to 4 hours. (Do not cook on HIGH.) Sprinkle with pecans; serve with whipped cream. Refrigerate leftovers. *Makes 6 to 8 servings*

Note: Store leftover cake in a covered container in the refrigerator. To serve leftover cake, reheat individual servings in the microwave for about 15 seconds. Or, make fudge truffles: roll leftover cake into small balls and dip them into melted chocolate. Let sit until chocolate hardens.

Poached Pears with Raspberry Sauce

Cook Time: 3½ to 4 hours

4 cups cran-raspberry juice cocktail

2 cups Rhine or Riesling wine

¼ cup sugar

2 cinnamon sticks, broken into halves

4 to 5 firm Bosc or Anjou pears, peeled and cored

1 package (10 ounces) frozen raspberries in syrup, thawed

Fresh berries (optional)

1. Combine juice, wine, sugar and cinnamon stick halves in slow cooker. Submerge pears in mixture. Cover; cook on LOW 3½ to 4 hours or until pears are tender. Remove and discard cinnamon sticks.

2. Process raspberries in food processor or blender until smooth; strain and discard seeds. Spoon raspberry sauce onto serving plates; place pear on top of sauce. Garnish with fresh berries, if desired.

Makes 4 to 5 servings

Pecan-Cinnamon Pudding Cake

Prep Time: 20 minutes **Cook Time:** 2 to 2½ hours (HIGH) **Stand Time:** 30 minutes

1⅓ cups all-purpose flour

½ cup granulated sugar

1½ teaspoons baking powder

1½ teaspoons ground cinnamon

⅔ cup milk

5 tablespoons butter, melted, divided

1 cup chopped pecans

1½ cups water

¾ cup packed brown sugar

Whipped cream (optional)

1. Stir together flour, granulated sugar, baking powder and cinnamon in medium bowl. Add milk and 3 tablespoons butter; mix just until blended. Stir in pecans. Spread on bottom of slow cooker.

2. Combine water, brown sugar and remaining 2 tablespoons butter in small saucepan; bring to a boil. Pour over batter in slow cooker.

3. Cover; cook on HIGH 2 to 2½ hours or until toothpick inserted into center of cake comes out clean. Let stand, uncovered, for 30 minutes. Serve warm with whipped cream, if desired.

Makes 8 servings

Apple-Date Crisp

Cook Time: 4 hours

6 cups thinly sliced peeled apples (about 6 medium apples, preferably Golden Delicious)

2 teaspoons lemon juice

⅓ cup chopped dates

1⅓ cups uncooked quick oats

½ cup all-purpose flour

½ cup packed light brown sugar

½ teaspoon ground cinnamon

¼ teaspoon ground ginger

¼ teaspoon salt

Dash ground nutmeg

Dash ground cloves (optional)

¼ cup (½ stick) cold butter, cut into small pieces

1. Spray slow cooker with nonstick cooking spray. Place apples in medium bowl. Sprinkle with lemon juice; toss to coat. Add dates and mix well. Transfer apple mixture to slow cooker.

2. Combine oats, flour, brown sugar, cinnamon, ginger, salt, nutmeg and cloves, if desired, in medium bowl. Cut in butter with pastry blender or two knives until mixture resembles coarse crumbs.

3. Sprinkle oat mixture over apples; smooth top. Cover; cook on LOW about 4 hours or on HIGH about 2 hours or until apples are tender.

Makes 6 servings

Pineapple Daiquiri Sundae

Cook Time: 3 to 4 hours (HIGH)

1 pineapple, cored, peeled and cut into ½-inch chunks

½ cup dark rum

½ cup sugar

3 tablespoons lime juice

Peel of 2 limes, cut in long strands

1 tablespoon cornstarch

Place all ingredients in 1½-quart slow cooker; mix well. Cover; cook on HIGH 3 to 4 hours. Serve hot over ice cream, pound cake or shortcakes. Garnish with a few fresh raspberries and mint leaves, if desired.

Makes 4 to 6 servings

Variation: Substitute 1 can (20 ounces) crushed pineapple, drained, for the fresh pineapple. Cook on HIGH 3 hours.

Pumpkin-Cranberry Custard

Cook Time: 4 to 4½ hours (HIGH)

1 can (30 ounces) pumpkin pie
    filling

1 can (12 ounces) evaporated
    milk

1 cup dried cranberries

4 eggs, lightly beaten

1 cup crushed or whole ginger
    snap cookies (optional)

    Whipped cream (optional)

Combine pumpkin, evaporated milk, cranberries and eggs in slow cooker; mix thoroughly. Cover; cook on HIGH 4 to 4½ hours. Serve with crushed or whole ginger snaps and whipped cream, if desired.

Make 4 to 6 servings

Peach Cobbler

Cook Time: 2 hours (HIGH)

2 packages (16 ounces each)
    frozen peaches, thawed and
    drained

¾ cup plus 1 tablespoon sugar,
    divided

2 teaspoons ground cinnamon,
    divided

½ teaspoon ground nutmeg

¾ cup all-purpose flour

6 tablespoons butter, cut into
    bits

    Whipped cream (if desired)

1. Combine peaches, ¾ cup sugar, 1½ teaspoons cinnamon and nutmeg in medium bowl. Place into slow cooker.

2. For topping, combine flour, remaining 1 tablespoon sugar and remaining ½ teaspoon cinnamon in separate bowl. Cut in butter with pastry blender or 2 knives until mixture resembles coarse crumbs. Sprinkle over peach mixture. Cover; cook on HIGH 2 hours. Serve with freshly whipped cream, if desired.

Makes 4 to 6 servings

Chocolate Chip Lemon Loaf

Cook Time: 3 to 4 hours

¾ cup granulated sugar

½ cup shortening

2 eggs

1⅔ cups all-purpose flour

1½ teaspoons baking powder

¼ teaspoon salt

¾ cup milk

½ cup chocolate chips

Grated peel of 1 lemon

Juice of 1 lemon

¼ to ½ cup powdered sugar

Melted chocolate (optional)

1. Turn slow cooker on LOW. Grease 2-quart soufflé dish; set aside. Beat granulated sugar and shortening in large bowl until blended. Add eggs, one at a time, mixing well after each addition.

2. Sift together flour, baking powder and salt. Add flour mixture and milk alternately to shortening mixture. Stir in chocolate chips and lemon peel.

3. Spoon batter into prepared dish. Cover with greased foil. Place in preheated slow cooker. Cook, covered, with slow cooker lid slightly ajar to allow excess moisture to escape, on LOW 3 to 4 hours or on HIGH 1¾ to 2 hours or until edges are golden and knife inserted into center of loaf comes out clean. Remove dish from slow cooker; remove foil. Place loaf on wire rack to cool completely.

4. Combine lemon juice and ¼ cup powdered sugar in small bowl until smooth. Add more sugar as needed to reach desired glaze consistency. Pour glaze over loaf. Drizzle loaf with melted chocolate, if desired.

Makes 8 servings

Steamed Southern Sweet Potato Custard

Cook Time: 2½ to 3 hours (HIGH)   **Stand Time:** 30 minutes

1 can (16 ounces) cut sweet
   potatoes, drained
1 can (12 ounces) evaporated
   milk, divided
½ cup packed light brown sugar
2 eggs, lightly beaten
1 teaspoon ground cinnamon
½ teaspoon ground ginger
¼ teaspoon salt
   Whipped cream
   Ground nutmeg

1. Process sweet potatoes with ¼ cup evaporated milk in food processor or blender until smooth. Add remaining milk, brown sugar, eggs, cinnamon, ginger and salt; process until well mixed. Pour into ungreased 1-quart soufflé dish. Cover tightly with foil. Crumple large sheet (about 15×12 inches) of foil; place in bottom of slow cooker. Pour 2 cups water over foil. Make foil handles.*

2. Transfer dish to slow cooker using foil handles. Cover; cook on HIGH 2½ to 3 hours or until skewer inserted into center comes out clean.

3. Using foil strips, lift dish from slow cooker; transfer to wire rack. Uncover; let stand 30 minutes. Garnish with whipped cream and nutmeg.   *Makes 4 servings*

To make foil handles, tear off three 18×3-inch strips of heavy-duty foil. Crisscross the strips so they resemble the spokes of a wheel. Place the dish in the center of the strips. Pull the foil strips up and over the dish and place it into the slow cooker. Leave the foil strips in while the food cooks, so you can easily lift the item out again when it is finished cooking.

Cherry Flan

Prep Time: 10 minutes   **Cook Time:** 3½ to 4 hours

5 eggs
½ cup sugar
½ teaspoon salt
¾ cup flour
1 can (12 ounces) evaporated milk
1 teaspoon vanilla
1 bag (16 ounces) frozen, pitted dark sweet cherries, thawed

1. Grease inside of slow cooker.

2. Beat eggs, sugar and salt in large bowl of electric mixer at high speed until thick. Add flour; beat until smooth. Beat in evaporated milk and vanilla.

3. Pour batter into prepared slow cooker. Place cherries evenly over batter. Cover; cook on LOW 3½ to 4 hours or until flan is set. Serve warm.   *Makes 6 servings*

Note: This yummy dessert is best served warm and is especially delicious when topped with whipped cream or ice cream.

Mixed Berry Cobbler

Prep Time: 10 minutes   **Cook Time:** 4 hours   **Stand Time:** 30 minutes

1 package (16 ounces) frozen mixed berries
¾ cup granulated sugar
2 tablespoons quick-cooking tapioca
2 teaspoons grated fresh lemon peel
1½ cups all-purpose flour
½ cup packed brown sugar
2¼ teaspoons baking powder
¼ teaspoon ground nutmeg
¾ cup milk
⅓ cup butter, melted
Ice cream (optional)

1. Stir together berries, granulated sugar, tapioca and lemon peel in slow cooker.

2. Combine flour, brown sugar, baking powder and nutmeg in medium bowl. Add milk and butter; stir just until blended. Drop spoonfuls on top of berry mixture.

3. Cover; cook on LOW 4 hours. Uncover; let stand about 30 minutes. Serve with ice cream, if desired.   *Makes 8 servings*

Peach-Pecan Upside-Down Cake

Prep Time: 10 minutes   **Cook Time:** 3 hours (HIGH)

1 can (8½ ounces) peach slices

⅓ cup packed brown sugar

2 tablespoons butter or margarine, melted

¼ cup chopped pecans

1 package (16 ounces) pound cake mix, plus ingredients to prepare mix

½ teaspoon almond extract

Whipped cream (optional)

1. Generously grease 7½-inch slow cooker bread-and-cake bake pan or casserole dish; set aside.

2. Drain peach slices, reserving 1 tablespoon of juice. Combine reserved peach juice, brown sugar and butter in prepared bake pan. Arrange peach slices on top of brown sugar mixture. Sprinkle with pecans.

3. Prepare cake mix according to package directions; stir in almond extract. Spread over peach mixture. Cover pan. Make foil handles (see Note page 240) for easier removal of pan from slow cooker. Place pan into slow cooker. Cover; cook on HIGH 3 hours.

4. Use foil handles to remove pan from slow cooker. Cool, uncovered, on wire rack for 10 minutes. Run narrow spatula around sides of pan; invert onto serving plate. Serve warm with whipped cream, if desired.

Makes 10 servings

Steamed Pumpkin Cake

Prep Time: 15 minutes   **Cook Time:** 3 to 3½ hours (HIGH)

1½ cups all-purpose flour

1½ teaspoons baking powder

1½ teaspoons baking soda

1 teaspoon ground cinnamon

½ teaspoon salt

¼ teaspoon ground cloves

½ cup unsalted butter, melted

2 cups packed light brown sugar

3 eggs, beaten

1 can (15 ounces) solid-pack pumpkin

Sweetened whipped cream (optional)

1. Grease 2½-quart soufflé dish or baking pan that fits into slow cooker.

2. Combine flour, baking powder, baking soda, cinnamon, salt and cloves in medium bowl; set aside.

3. Beat butter, brown sugar and eggs in large bowl with electric mixer on medium speed until creamy. Beat in pumpkin. Stir in flour mixture. Spoon batter into prepared soufflé dish.

4. Fill slow cooker with 1-inch hot water. Make foil handles using technique described below to allow for easy removal of soufflé dish. Place soufflé dish into slow cooker. Cover; cook on HIGH 3 to 3½ hours or until wooden toothpick inserted into center comes out clean.

5. Use foil handles to lift dish from slow cooker. Cool 15 minutes. Invert cake onto serving platter. Cut into wedges and serve with dollop of whipped cream, if desired.

Makes 12 servings

Foil Handles: Tear off three 18×2-inch strips of heavy foil or use regular foil folded to double thickness. Crisscross foil strips in spoke design and place soufflé dish on center of strips. Pull foil strips up and over dish.

Serving Suggestion: Enhance this old-fashioned dense cake with a topping of sautéed apples or pear slices, or a scoop of pumpkin ice cream.

MY FAVORITES

My Favorite Recipes

Favorite recipe: _____

Favorite recipe from: _____

Ingredients: _____

_____

_____

_____

_____

_____

Method: _____

_____

_____

_____

_____

_____

_____

_____

_____

_____

_____

My Favorite Recipes

Favorite recipe: _____

Favorite recipe from: _____

Ingredients: _____

_____

_____

_____

_____

Method: _____

_____

_____

_____

_____

_____

_____

_____

_____

My Favorite Recipes

Favorite recipe: _____

Favorite recipe from: _____

Ingredients: _____

_____

_____

_____

_____

_____

Method: _____

_____

_____

_____

_____

_____

_____

_____

_____

_____

_____

My Favorite Recipes

Favorite recipe: _____

Favorite recipe from: _____

Ingredients: _____

_____

_____

_____

_____

_____

Method: _____

_____

_____

_____

_____

_____

_____

_____

_____

_____

My Favorite Recipes

Favorite recipe: _____

Favorite recipe from: _____

Ingredients: _____

_____

_____

_____

_____

_____

Method: _____

_____

_____

_____

_____

_____

_____

_____

_____

_____

_____

My Favorite Recipes

Favorite recipe: _____

Favorite recipe from: _____

Ingredients: _____

_____

_____

_____

_____

_____

Method: _____

_____

_____

_____

_____

_____

_____

_____

_____

_____

_____

My Favorite Recipes

Favorite recipe: _____

Favorite recipe from: _____

Ingredients: _____

_____

_____

_____

_____

_____

Method: _____

_____

_____

_____

_____

_____

_____

_____

_____

_____

_____

My Favorite Recipes

Favorite recipe: _____

Favorite recipe from: _____

Ingredients: _____

_____

_____

_____

_____

Method: _____

_____

_____

_____

_____

_____

_____

_____

_____

_____

My Favorite Recipes

Favorite recipe: _____

Favorite recipe from: _____

Ingredients: _____

_____

_____

_____

_____

_____

Method: _____

_____

_____

_____

_____

_____

_____

_____

_____

_____

_____

_____

My Favorite Recipes

Favorite recipe: _____

Favorite recipe from: _____

Ingredients: _____

_____

_____

_____

_____

Method: _____

_____

_____

_____

_____

_____

_____

_____

_____

_____

My Favorite Dinner Party

Date: _____

Occasion: _____
_____

Guests: _____
_____
_____
_____
_____

Menu: _____
_____
_____
_____
_____
_____
_____
_____
_____
_____
_____

My Favorite Dinner Party

Date: _____

Occasion: _____

_____

Guests: _____

_____

_____

_____

_____

Menu: _____

_____

_____

_____

_____

_____

_____

_____

_____

_____

My Favorite Dinner Party

Date: _____

Occasion: _____

_____

Guests: _____

_____

_____

_____

Menu: _____

_____

_____

_____

_____

_____

_____

_____

_____

My Favorite Dinner Party

Date: _____

Occasion: _____

_____

Guests: _____

_____

_____

_____

_____

Menu: _____

_____

_____

_____

_____

_____

_____

_____

_____

_____

_____

My Favorite Dinner Party

Date: _____

Occasion: _____
_____

Guests: _____
_____
_____
_____
_____

Menu: _____
_____
_____
_____
_____
_____
_____
_____
_____

My Favorite Dinner Party

Date: _____

Occasion: _____

_____

Guests: _____

_____

_____

_____

_____

Menu: _____

_____

_____

_____

_____

_____

_____

_____

_____

_____

_____

My Favorite Dinner Party

Date: _____

Occasion: _____

_____

Guests: _____

_____

_____

_____

_____

Menu: _____

_____

_____

_____

_____

_____

_____

_____

_____

_____

My Favorite Dinner Party

Date: _____

Occasion: _____

_____

Guests: _____

_____

_____

_____

Menu: _____

_____

_____

_____

_____

_____

_____

_____

_____

_____

My Favorite Pot-Luck Recipes

Favorite recipe: _____

Favorite recipe from: _____

Ingredients: _____

_____

_____

_____

_____

_____

Method: _____

_____

_____

_____

_____

_____

_____

_____

_____

_____

_____

My Favorite Pot-Luck Recipes

Favorite recipe: _____

Favorite recipe from: _____

Ingredients: _____

_____

_____

_____

_____

Method: _____

_____

_____

_____

_____

_____

_____

_____

_____

_____

My Favorite Pot-Luck Recipes

Favorite recipe: _____

Favorite recipe from: _____

Ingredients: _____

_____

_____

_____

_____

_____

Method: _____

_____

_____

_____

_____

_____

_____

_____

_____

_____

_____

My Favorite Pot-Luck Recipes

Favorite recipe: _____

Favorite recipe from: _____

Ingredients: _____

_____

_____

_____

_____

_____

Method: _____

_____

_____

_____

_____

_____

_____

_____

_____

_____

_____

_____

My Favorite Weeknight Meals

Favorite recipe: _____

Favorite recipe from: _____

Ingredients: _____

_____

_____

_____

_____

_____

Method: _____

_____

_____

_____

_____

_____

_____

_____

_____

_____

_____

My Favorite Weeknight Meals

Favorite recipe: _____

Favorite recipe from: _____

Ingredients: _____

_____

_____

_____

_____

_____

Method: _____

_____

_____

_____

_____

_____

_____

_____

_____

_____

My Favorite Weeknight Meals

Favorite recipe: _____

Favorite recipe from: _____

Ingredients: _____

_____

_____

_____

_____

Method: _____

_____

_____

_____

_____

_____

_____

_____

_____

_____

My Favorite Weeknight Meals

Favorite recipe: _____

Favorite recipe from: _____

Ingredients: _____

_____

_____

_____

_____

_____

Method: _____

_____

_____

_____

_____

_____

_____

_____

_____

_____

My Favorite Friends

Friend: _____

Favorite foods: _____

_____

_____

_____

_____

Don't serve: _____

_____

_____

_____

_____

_____

_____

_____

_____

_____

My Favorite Friends

Friend: _____

Favorite foods: _____

_____

_____

_____

_____

Don't serve: _____

_____

_____

_____

_____

_____

_____

_____

_____

_____

_____

_____

_____

My Favorite Friends

Friend: _____

Favorite foods: _____

_____

_____

_____

_____

Don't serve: _____

_____

_____

_____

_____

_____

_____

_____

_____

_____

_____

My Favorite Friends

Friend: _____

Favorite foods: _____

_____

_____

_____

_____

Don't serve: _____

_____

_____

_____

_____

_____

_____

_____

_____

_____

_____

_____

My Favorite Friends

Friend: _____

Favorite foods: _____

_____

_____

_____

_____

Don't serve: _____

_____

_____

_____

_____

_____

_____

_____

_____

_____

_____

My Favorite Friends

Friend: _____

Favorite foods: _____

_____

_____

_____

_____

Don't serve: _____

_____

_____

_____

_____

_____

_____

_____

_____

_____

_____

_____

_____

_____

HINTS, TIPS
& INDEX

Slow Cooker Hints and Tips

The slow cooker is one of the most popular appliances in today's kitchen—and for good reason. What other appliance allows you to start dinner in the morning, then gives you the freedom to enjoy your day far from your kitchen? And when you arrive home, a hot savory dinner is waiting. You can easily take a slow-cooked dinner to a potluck supper and keep it warm for several hours. When entertaining you can rely on your slow cooker to free up a burner or leave valuable oven space for another item on your menu. Plus, cleanup is quick and easy. No wonder versatile slow cookers are loved by cooks across America.

How Does a Slow Cooker Work?

A slow cooker is usually a metal container with a heavy ceramic insert.

Inserts have either a clear glass or plastic cover. Most inserts are removable for easy cleaning.

There are two general types of slow cookers. The most common type has heating coils that circle the outer container producing heat on either a low or high setting. The low setting is generally about 200°F and the high setting is about 300°F. Food is placed in the insert, covered and heated by the slow steady heat produced by the coils. The recipes in this book were developed and tested with this type of slow cooker. The second type has heating coils under the insert that cycle on and off. The recipes in this book have not been tested with this type of appliance; refer to the manufacturer's directions for guidance with cooking times and temperature settings.

The slow cooking process creates steam. Since the slow cooker is covered throughout the cooking process, the steam can't escape. Instead, it condenses to form liquid that returns to the food. The amount of liquid in the food increases during cooking, so don't be surprised if there doesn't seem to be enough liquid when you begin cooking.

Slow cookers require very little energy, making them economical appliances to use. In addition, they don't heat the kitchen, so they are a good choice for cooking on hot summer days.

What Slow Cookers Do Best

Slow cookers are ideal for making soups, stews and chilis, dishes that require long cooking. Slow cooking allows the flavors of the meat or poultry and vegetables to develop and blend. And long slow cooking tenderizes the toughest cuts of meat.

Slow cookers are useful when entertaining. When used to prepare one of the dishes on the menu, a slow cooker will free up a burner or space in the oven for something else. And the slow-cooked dish gives you more time to concentrate on other menu items. A slow cooker can also be used to keep food hot on a buffet table. Whether it's hot mulled cider, a warm artichoke dip or a main dish, your slow cooker can save the day.

Prepare your favorite slow-cooked hot dish and carry it to a potluck dinner. (Special carriers are made for just this

purpose.) Desserts, such as fruit dishes, pudding and custards, can be prepared in a slow cooker. Surprisingly, even cakes can be made in this appliance. You'll find that these cakes are moist, because they've been steamed. They can be made right in the ceramic insert or in a special cake pan offered by one manufacturer. Pudding cakes, moist cakes with pudding underneath, also work well in a slow cooker.

Slow Cooker Tips and Techniques

If you have not used a slow cooker, the following tips and techniques will help you get started and give you a clear understanding of the world of slow cooking. If you're an old hand at slow cooking, browse through the list of techniques and you might find the solution to a problem you've experienced. Or, you might discover something new that will enhance your slow cooking experience and turn you into an expert.

Tenderizing

Since slow cooking is an effective way to tenderize meat, tougher cuts of meat—which have more flavor than lean cuts—are an excellent choice. Cuts like brisket, chuck roast, rump roast, stew meat, pork spareribs and pork shoulder become fork-tender when cooked in a slow cooker. But the selection in this cookbook isn't limited to just these cuts; you'll find some of the convenient choices you love, such as flank steak, ground beef and turkey, sausage and pork chops.

Browning Meat and Poultry

While not necessary, browning meat before slow cooking does have benefits. You've probably noticed that searing meat on a grill or in a skillet produces wonderful aromas and distinctive flavors that make steaks, burgers and chops extra special. The flavor produced by browning will add complexity to slow-cooked beef, pork and lamb meals. Ground beef and poultry should always be browned and drained of fat before placing them in the slow cooker. Browning also gives meat a more pleasant color.

Preparing Poultry

Chicken skin tends to shrivel and curl in the slow cooker, so most recipes call for skinless chicken. If you prefer to use skin-on pieces, brown them in a skillet before adding them to the slow cooker. Remove excess fat from poultry before cooking it. A whole chicken is too large to cook safely in a slow cooker; always cut a whole chicken into quarters or individual pieces before cooking it.

Preparing Vegetables

Vegetables, especially root vegetables, can take longer to cook than meats. Cut vegetables into uniform pieces so they finish cooking at the same time. Root vegetables, like potatoes, carrots and turnips, should be cut into small pieces and placed on the bottom of the slow cooker so they are always submerged in liquid. Vegetables usually do not need to be precooked. Occasionally a recipe will call for sautéing onions and garlic before slow cooking; this is done to reduce their sharpness. For example, in French Onion Soup (page 16), the onions are sautéed long enough to allow them to develop a caramelized flavor, which adds a very distinctive note to the finished soup.

Strong-flavored vegetables, such as broccoli, cabbage and cauliflower, may be added during the last hour or two of cooking to prevent their flavor from overwhelming the dish. Tender, delicate vegetables, such as spinach, green onions and snow peas, should also be added during the last hour of cooking to prevent overcooking them.

Dairy Products

Long slow cooking (4 hours or more) can make dairy products curdle or separate. Add milk, cream, sour cream and cheese during the last 15 to 30 minutes of cooking. Certain dairy products can be used successfully because they have undergone high heat processing. Examples of these are processed cheese and evaporated milk, which can be safely added early in the cooking process. Condensed soups can also withstand long cooking without breaking down.

Boosting Flavor

When foods cook for a long time, dried herbs and some spices tend to diminish in flavor, resulting in a bland dish. As more steam condenses in the slow cooker and the liquid in the dish increases, flavors become diluted. (Conventional cooking, on the other hand, results in evaporation of liquid and seasonings tend to become stronger the longer they are cooked.) To correct this problem, always taste the dish about 30 minutes before the end of the cooking time and add additional herbs and spices as needed.

Controlling the Heat of Pepper

Some spices tend to increase in flavor during long cooking. The best examples of this are black and red pepper, which can become very harsh and extra spicy during long cooking. If you or a family member is sensitive to heat from pepper, use less than the recipe suggests or wait until the last 30 minutes to add it.

Improving the Appearance of the Finished Dish

Long cooking can result in vegetables losing their bright color, so finished dishes may look washed out. To avoid this, add delicate vegetables near the

end of cooking. Another option is to garnish the dish before serving. Garnishes like chopped green onions, chopped parsley, chopped fresh tomatoes, shredded cheese, sour cream, lemon or lime wedges, and crisply cooked and crumbled bacon add just the touch of color needed. Be sure that the flavor of the garnish complements rather than detracts from the dish.

Make-Ahead Preparation

Mornings can be hectic times. If time is at a premium in the morning in your kitchen, you may find it easier to prepare ingredients the night before. For safety's sake, cover and refrigerate all items until ready to use. Also, keep vegetables in a separate bowl from meat and poultry. Do not brown meat or poultry the night before; partially cooking meat or poultry and refrigerating it allows bacteria to grow. Just before cooking, add the prepared ingredients to the slow cooker; you may need to add an extra 30 minutes to the cooking time because the ingredients will be very cold.

Filling the Slow Cooker

For best results, fill the slow cooker insert at least one-half full, but not more than three-quarters full. Many recipes recommend placing firm root vegetables on the bottom of the insert and the meat on top of the vegetables.

Slow Cooker Settings

Slow cookers have two settings, low and high. Most recipes can be cooked at either setting. Generally, 2 to 2½ hours on low equals 1 hour on high. Most of the recipes in this book give cooking times for both low and high settings. If the recipe only lists one heat setting, this is the only one that should be used. Cooking on the low setting may result in slightly better blending of flavors, and tough meats may become more tender when cooked on the low setting.

Another option for slow cooking is to cook for the first hour on the high setting, then reduce the heat to low to finish the dish. This reduces the total cooking time by one to two hours. Some slow cooker models offer a feature that automatically changes the heat setting to low after 1 hour on the high setting.

Keep the Lid On

A slow cooker can take as long as 30 minutes to regain heat lost when the cover is removed. Only remove the cover when instructed to do so in the recipe. Generally, slow cooker dishes seldom need stirring. With heating coils wrapped around the outside of the appliance and low heat, there's no danger of scorched food. If you can't resist the urge to peek in the slow cooker, tap the cover gently or spin it lightly to remove the condensation, then you should be able to see what's going on in the slow cooker.

Thickening Slow-Cooked Dishes

Thickeners are usually added during the last 15 to 30 minutes of cooking. The amount of liquid created in a slow cooker dish may vary from unit to unit. Cooking on the low heat setting results in more juices than cooking on high. Removing the cover repeatedly during cooking will reduce liquids. If there doesn't seem to be much liquid, it is best to use only a portion (one half to three fourths) of the listed amount of the thickening agent, adding more if necessary. If a dish becomes too thick, simply add additional broth or water to thin the sauce.

Low-Fat Techniques

One great advantage of slow cookers is that you can easily prepare low-fat meals in them. Since foods are not generally sautéed in butter or oil, the fat content is naturally lower in slow-cooked meals. To trim even more fat from slow cooker dishes, choose lean meat, trim excess fat, remove the skin from chicken and brown meat in a nonstick skillet, then drain fat from it. Or, slip meat under the broiler for a few minutes to brown it before adding it to the slow cooker. Any fat that does accumulate during cooking will rise to the surface and can be skimmed off before serving.

Baked Goods in a Slow Cooker:

If you wish to prepare bread, cakes or pudding cakes in a slow cooker, you may want to purchase a covered, vented metal cake pan accessory for your slow cooker. You can also use any straight sided soufflé dish or deep cake pan that will fit into the ceramic insert of your unit. Baked goods can be prepared directly in the insert; they can be a little difficult to remove from the insert, so follow the recipe directions carefully.

Slow Cooker Techniques for Special Foods

Frozen Foods

Avoid cooking frozen foods in a slow cooker. For food safety's sake, do not cook frozen meat or chicken in a slow cooker. Instead, thaw it in the refrigerator before cooking. It's best not to cook packages of frozen vegetables in a slow cooker; rather, thaw them before slow cooking or cook them conventionally. You may add small amounts ($1/2$ to 1 cup) of frozen vegetables, such as peas, green beans, broccoli florets and corn, to a slow-cooked meal during the last 30 to 45 minutes of cooking. Cook on the high setting until the vegetables are tender (you may need to add a few minutes to the cooking time).

Rice

Choose long-grain converted rice (or Arborio rice when suggested) or wild rice for best results. Long, slow cooking can turn other types of rice into mush; if you prefer to use other types of rice instead of converted rice, cook them conventionally and add them to the slow cooker during the last 15 minutes of cooking. However, you can add a small amount ($1/2$ cup) of uncooked rice to a slow cooker soup or other dish during the last hour of cooking; just be sure to add it to boiling liquid. If you wish to add uncooked rice to a recipe that doesn't include it, you will need to adjust the liquid as well. Add an equal amount of water or broth before you add the rice.

Pasta

Pasta needs to be cooked in a large quantity of boiling water; it should not be cooked in a slow cooker. However, you can add small amounts ($1/2$ to 1 cup) of small pasta, such as orzo, small shell macaroni, ditali and short lengths of linguine to boiling liquid during the last one hour of slow cooking. You may also cook pasta in boiling water and add it to the slow cooker during the last 30 minutes of cooking.

Fish

Fish cooks quickly and can easily be overcooked. That's why it requires special care when slow cooking. First, choose only firm white fish, such as cod, haddock, sea bass, red snapper or orange roughy. Avoid more delicate varieties and thin fillets because they will fall apart. If fish is frozen, thaw it overnight in the refrigerator in its original packaging before cooking it.

Shellfish

Shellfish, such as shrimp, scallops and oysters, are delicate and should be added to the slow cooker during the last 15 to 30 minutes of the cooking time. Use a high heat setting for shellfish. If you add a large quantity of shellfish to the slow cooker, you may need to add a little extra cooking time. Watch shellfish carefully; it overcooks easily.

Slow Cooker Safety

Food Safety

Food safety is always a concern when you're cooking and serving food. Organisms that cause food-borne illness thrive at temperatures between 40°F and 140°F. Research has shown that slow cookers, even on the low heat setting, raise the temperature of the food quickly through this danger zone, making them a safe way to cook.

Power Outages

If you arrive home and find the electrical power service to your home is out, check the slow cooker immediately. With an instant-read thermometer, check the temperature of the contents of the slow cooker. If the temperature is above 140°F, you can transfer the contents to a large saucepan or Dutch oven and finish cooking it on a gas range or gas grill. However, if the temperature of the contents is between 40°F and 140°F, you should throw the contents away.

If the electricity is on when you arrive home, but you can tell by the clocks that your home has been without power, the best thing to do is throw away the food. You will never know what the temperature of the food was when the power went off; it may have spent several hours in the danger zone. And, although it's hot when you get home and looks done, it is better to err on the side of safety.

Make-Ahead Safety

When you prepare ingredients ahead for later cooking, always refrigerate meat and poultry in a separate bowl from the vegetables. Do not store ingredients in the slow cooker insert; starting with a cold insert will lengthen the cooking time.

Frozen Foods Safety

Do not cook frozen meat or poultry in the slow cooker. It takes too long on either the low or high setting to go through the danger zone (40°F and 140°F), which gives organisms a perfect place to grow and multiply. Large amounts of frozen vegetables are best thawed before adding them to a slow cooker. However, small amounts of frozen vegetables can be added to the slow cooker (see Frozen Foods on page 278 for more information).

Meat and Poultry Safety

Never brown or partially cook meat or poultry, then refrigerate them for later cooking. Instead, cook them immediately after browning.

Cook meat and poultry thoroughly: At the end of the cooking time, check the temperatures of poultry, meat and meatballs using an instant read thermometer. Poultry should be 180°F, beef and pork 160° to 170°F and meatballs 165°F.

Appliance Safety

Some slow cookers have a warm setting designed to hold food above 145°F. To confirm that your slow cooker is working properly, check the temperature of the food periodically while it is on the warm setting. The temperature should not drop below 140°F.

Protect the electrical cord from nicks and cuts. Check the cord periodically; if you find nicks or cuts in the cord, replace it.

Handling Leftovers Safely

Refrigerate leftovers quickly. Food can stand in a slow cooker that is turned off for up to 1 hour. To quickly chill leftovers, divide them into several small containers rather one large container; they will chill faster and give bacteria less chance to grow. Do not reheat leftovers in a slow cooker. Instead, heat them on the top of the range or in a microwave oven.

Acknowledgments

The publisher would like to thank the companies
and organizations listed below for the use of their recipes
and photographs in this publication.

Cabot® Creamery Cooperative

Hormel Foods, LLC

Jennie-O Turkey Store®

National Pork Board

Reckitt Benckiser Inc.

Veg•All®

METRIC CONVERSION CHART

VOLUME MEASUREMENTS (dry)

$1/8$ teaspoon = 0.5 mL
$1/4$ teaspoon = 1 mL
$1/2$ teaspoon = 2 mL
$3/4$ teaspoon = 4 mL
1 teaspoon = 5 mL
1 tablespoon = 15 mL
2 tablespoons = 30 mL
$1/4$ cup = 60 mL
$1/3$ cup = 75 mL
$1/2$ cup = 125 mL
$2/3$ cup = 150 mL
$3/4$ cup = 175 mL
1 cup = 250 mL
2 cups = 1 pint = 500 mL
3 cups = 750 mL
4 cups = 1 quart = 1 L

VOLUME MEASUREMENTS (fluid)

1 fluid ounce (2 tablespoons) = 30 mL
4 fluid ounces ($1/2$ cup) = 125 mL
8 fluid ounces (1 cup) = 250 mL
12 fluid ounces ($1 1/2$ cups) = 375 mL
16 fluid ounces (2 cups) = 500 mL

WEIGHTS (mass)

$1/2$ ounce = 15 g
1 ounce = 30 g
3 ounces = 90 g
4 ounces = 120 g
8 ounces = 225 g
10 ounces = 285 g
12 ounces = 360 g
16 ounces = 1 pound = 450 g

DIMENSIONS

$1/16$ inch = 2 mm
$1/8$ inch = 3 mm
$1/4$ inch = 6 mm
$1/2$ inch = 1.5 cm
$3/4$ inch = 2 cm
1 inch = 2.5 cm

OVEN TEMPERATURES

250°F = 120°C
275°F = 140°C
300°F = 150°C
325°F = 160°C
350°F = 180°C
375°F = 190°C
400°F = 200°C
425°F = 220°C
450°F = 230°C

BAKING PAN SIZES

Utensil	Size in Inches/Quarts	Metric Volume	Size in Centimeters
Baking or Cake Pan (square or rectangular)	8×8×2	2 L	20×20×5
	9×9×2	2.5 L	23×23×5
	12×8×2	3 L	30×20×5
	13×9×2	3.5 L	33×23×5
Loaf Pan	8×4×3	1.5 L	20×10×7
	9×5×3	2 L	23×13×7
Round Layer Cake Pan	8×1½	1.2 L	20×4
	9×1½	1.5 L	23×4
Pie Plate	8×1¼	750 mL	20×3
	9×1¼	1 L	23×3
Baking Dish or Casserole	1 quart	1 L	—
	1½ quart	1.5 L	—
	2 quart	2 L	—